Blackout Girl

Blackout Girl

Growing Up and Drying Out in America

by Jennifer Storm

HAZELDEN

Hazelden
Center City, Minnesota 55012-0176
1-800-328-0094
1-651-213-4590 (Fax)
www.hazelden.org

Editor's note: Some people's names in this book have been changed to protect
their anonymity.

Alcoholics Anonymous and AA are registered trademarks of AA World Services.

Hazelden offers a variety of information on chemical dependency and
related areas. The views and interpretations expressed herein are those of
the author and are neither endorsed nor approved by AA or any Twelve Step
organization.

Cover design Theresa Gedig
Interior design and production David Farr, ImageSmythe

Library of Congress Cataloging-in-Publication Data

Storm, Jennifer, 1975–
    Blackout girl: growing up and drying out in America/by Jennifer Storm.
        p. cm.
    ISBN 978-1-59285-468-4 (softcover)
    1. Storm, Jennifer, 1975– 2. Women alcoholics—United States—Biography.
3. Women drug addicts—United States—Biography. I. Title.
    HV5293.S76S76 2008
    362.29092—dc22
    [B]

                                                                2007040998

11 10 09 08   2 3 4 5 6

Dedication

This book is dedicated to my Higher Power and the people
in the rooms of Alcoholics Anonymous, for without the
combination of these two powerful entities in my life,
I would not be here. To the alcoholic or addict who is
still sick and suffering, may this book read as a guide to
recovery for whatever you are going through. May you
find hope in these pages.

Contents

Blackout Girl

Preface

WHEN I WAS FIRST APPROACHED with the idea of titling this book *Blackout Girl*, I have to admit, I was slightly offended—mainly, because I haven't blacked out in more than ten years, so it just doesn't seem to fit with who I am today. As a teen and young adult, though, I blacked out all the time. I *was* the blackout girl, the one at every party who drank too much, never knew when to say no, and called you the next day asking you to tell me what happened the night before. I awoke many times to my first thoughts being "Where the hell am I?" "How did I get here?" and "Where is my car?" So I guess the book's title is fitting for the story. Just don't expect me to respond to "Hey, Blackout Girl!" if you see me on the street now.

Before you read further, I want to define *blackout* in my own terms for you, because there are many misperceptions about it. Many people think *blacking out* and *passing out* are interchangeable terms. They are not. Passing out is something you do when you are extremely tired and your body just gives out and you fall asleep, or when you have drunk so much, taken so many pills, or done so many drugs that you pass out from them—passing out being a sleeping state.

Blacking out is totally different. Blacking out occurs when you lose conscious thought, control over motion and time. Blacking out usually occurs when a person drinks way too much, is deeply traumatized, or has some medical condition. *Merriam-Webster's Collegiate Dictionary* defines the verb *black out* in several ways, but these two I feel are the most applicable definitions: "to become enveloped in darkness or to undergo a temporary loss of vision, consciousness, or memory."

The vast difference is that when a person is in a blackout, he or she can very well be wide awake. He can be talking, granted, sometimes slurring and not making much sense, but talking nonetheless. She can be moving, driving, dancing. The person can be in motion of some kind but without the cognitive reasoning behind the actions or the ability to control them. And in many cases, that person cannot and will not remember any of it afterward. A blackout may also involve totally losing consciousness. I have had varying experiences, but regardless of how they took form, whether I was out cold and motionless or crazy in motion, they were all blackouts. I should know, because I have had many.

My first blackout came the first time I drank. I drank a lot, too much, and I blacked out, leaving me with a dark, empty space in my mind where the memory should have been. Other times, I would be left with bits and pieces of a memory. It was like a film playing in my head that felt sort of familiar, as though maybe I had seen it before, but some of the scenes had been switched around or edited out altogether.

Or you might say it's like opening an old jigsaw puzzle, dumping the contents on the table, and finding there are only five pieces of the 100-piece puzzle. And when you check the front of the box to see what the picture is supposed to be, it is too worn to make out.

To this day, I still have many memories that are shattered, with pieces lying throughout my past, whether in other memories or buried deep within myself. I am still trying to fit some of those pieces into place. Many are lost and I will never have complete pictures or full recollections of some of the events in my past. You will not read any lengthy conversations in this book, because there is no way for me to recall that level of detail for the past experiences I had when I was under the influence.

Because I wanted this book to be as rigorously honest as possible, certain details aren't here simply because of the blackout factor. Everything you read in the following pages is true to the best of my recollection and perception of events in my life, without exaggeration or embellishment. I have changed many names to protect those who have crossed my path; however, I have not altered the facts I know in any way.

This is my life as I have experienced and remember it. To put it mildly, I have lived a very colorful life in my thirty-some years on the planet. I feel blessed for all I have seen and grateful to be alive to tell my stories. Writing this book has helped me collect a couple of those missing memory pieces, and I am thankful to be in a position to share them with you.

Acknowledgments

I WISH TO THANK MY FATHER, who did the best job he could raising me and providing for me. Your love and support throughout the years have enabled me to become the person I am today. I thank you and love you so much. You are my hero. To my stepmother, who has been an angel to me and in many ways saved me, I cherish and love you. My brothers Brian and Jimmy for providing me with constant laughter and unconditional love and support. I love you both so much. To my sponsor, who is truly a daily reflection of me. You are my mentor, my big sister, and my best friend. I love you! To Danaca Clark for your amazing unconditional love and support of me throughout the years. You are such a blessing in my life. To my niece, Cheyanne, who serves as the other daily reflection of me. You are my angel eyes; I adore you! To Dawn Junk, who provided me with the encouragement and space to write much of this book, I thank you for that and so much more.

My Roma, my best friend, my partner, and my love. Thank you!

To my amazing staff and board who have supported me unconditionally, thank you for all that you have given me. To all my friends along the way—you have each touched my life in very special ways. I am eternally grateful to each and every one of you. I have learned so much through my interactions with each of you. I carry a piece of those experiences with me daily, and they are interwoven into the very fabric of who I am today. Thank you and peace be with you.

Introduction

I CLIMB OUT OF MY NEW SUV and close the door. I am wrapping my black wool coat tightly around me and checking the time on my BlackBerry when my tired colleague joins me on the sidewalk. It's 4:15 A.M. and we have been out for about three hours. "What was the address Detective Carter gave you?" I ask. She pulls out a small piece of paper and reads off the address.

I am not fazed to be on a dark street in a bad neighborhood in the middle of the night, because I've done that plenty of times in my sordid past, but this time is different. My purpose for being here is different. As we locate the house, I am keenly aware of how ironic this situation is. I walk up the cement steps and knock loudly on the door. I hold my breath and silently say a prayer. "God, please be my voice; allow me to deliver this message with compassion and love. God, please be with me and them."

The door opens and a frail, older black woman in pajamas appears. "Good morning, Ma'am. Are you Mrs. Hunt, Jamie Hunt's mother?" I ask. Her eyes widen as she stutters out a "yes." "My name is Jennifer Storm, and I am the executive director of the Victim/Witness Assistance Program. This is my colleague Amy. May we please come in, Ma'am?" She nods and opens the door for us to enter. In the living room, a small child plays on the steps. The woman says to an older man, "Honey, these people are from the county." He looks at us cautiously, realizing that we are not there with good news. He motions to the child to go upstairs. She pouts and gives me a dirty look as she stomps up the stairs. "What is this regarding?" he asks. Mrs. Hunt has taken a seat on the couch, and Amy sits down next to her. I ask Mr. Hunt if he would like to sit down, and he quickly responds that he is fine. I can tell he is half scared and half annoyed that we are in his home at this early hour. I kneel down in front of Mrs. Hunt.

This is the part of my job that I dislike the most. It is the hardest thing a person can do, yet I do it with such ease that it almost frightens me. My voice goes into a very gentle but concise tone as I say, "At approximately 11:30 P.M., your son Jamie was shot twice on North Third Street in downtown Harrisburg." Her eyes widen and she gasps as her husband raises his hand to his forehead. I don't miss a beat, as I know I have to get this next sentence out as soon as I can. "He died instantly." Mrs. Hunt begins to let out a piercing scream that cuts the air like a knife. Amy immediately puts her arms around her and attempts to console her. Mr. Hunt quickly goes into the next room, shaking his head briskly back and forth, and he just mutters over and over again, "No, this can't be. No, I just saw my son tonight. No, it isn't possible." His desperate eyes meet mine and he says, "Are you sure it was Jamie? I was just with him." I meet his eyes directly and respond, "Yes, sir. We are positive. The coroner made a positive identification thirty minutes ago. Here is his number for you to call." I continue to hold his gaze and tell him how sorry I am for his loss as I hand him the business card.

I explain that his son's body is at the coroner's office until the autopsy is done. They will then transport the body to whatever funeral parlor the family prefers. I go into detail about what our agency does, how we can help with the funeral arrangements. I tell them about victim's compensation and that financial assistance is available should they need it. I watch his face as I have watched the faces of so many parents in disbelief. I know he is only half hearing me because he is in shock.

Mrs. Hunt is in the other room on the phone calling relatives and screaming into the phone, "They killed my baby. Jamie is gone. They killed him. Jamie was shot. You need to come over here right now." Amy and I stay while family members begin to arrive. They have a ton of questions, some we can answer and some we cannot. What happened? Where was he? What was he doing? I know the answers to some of the questions and give as many facts as I can. I also know that Jamie was there to buy drugs, and it was a bad neighborhood, but I do not offer that information. They probably know that already, and it isn't the time or place to say it.

We leave them plenty of materials detailing our agency's services, information they will need for the upcoming months, about the criminal justice process and what happens when the offender is caught. After an hour or so, the family clearly needs to be alone, so Amy and I give our condolences once more and let them know they can call us anytime, twenty-four hours a day.

As we walk out of the house, I am exhausted inside. I look over at Amy, who has the same withered expression on her face that I know I do. We just shake our heads and get back into my car. I feel the sense of irony again, realizing anew that the body I saw a couple of hours ago could have been my body. The blood spilling out over the sidewalk could have been my blood. The parents opening their door could have been my parents.

Many years ago, I ran the streets in the middle of the night buying drugs, risking my life to get high. But not today. Today I am the person who does the knocking and delivers the message no parent or person should ever have to hear.

Blackout Girl

1

Tracing Scars

I HAVE A SCAR DIRECTLY UNDER MY CHIN that I got when I was a young child. My brother Brian and I were playing horsey around the large wooden coffee table in our living room. Brian thought it would be funny to push me as I was rounding the table, and my chin smashed right into its sharp corner. A couple of years later, that same brother thought it would be even funnier to see what a sparkler would look like directly on my right arm, producing a very large scar near the bend in my elbow.

But the worst scars are those that came from my own decisions. Decisions...I have made many bad decisions in my life.

The scar on my left knee came from practicing my back dive on the side of the pool one time, curving all the way over to the left and sliding down along the pool's concrete side into the water, scraping the skin off my knee. Ouch!

Then there is the tiny scar between my eyes that was caused by a nasty girl at a dance club one night. She apparently didn't appreciate the fact that I was drunk and making out with her boyfriend, so she smashed a sixteen-ounce glass into my face.

Finally there are the scars on my wrists. These are probably the most painful scars I have. They are deep and violently race across both wrists like a road map of hopelessness. One day I woke up in the mental ward of St. Luke's Hospital with three doctors standing over me, my wrists tightly wrapped in bright white gauze with a splint on the left hand to hold my wrist and my hand together. In that moment, I didn't want to die anymore—after my decision to die, I made the decision to live. It's been more than ten years since then.

No matter the story, each scar carries pain, reminders, laughter, and tears. Every time I look at them, they serve as vivid reminders of who I am and where I have been. Reminders of the good, the bad, and the downright ugly, even when I can't remember all the details of how I got them. These downright ugly scars keep me sane and sober today, reminding me of how bad it was and how bad it can be and how today, well, how good it is and will be tomorrow, too. The scars of yesterday not only remind me of the past but help carry me through the present and give me hope for the future.

2

First Beer, First Blackout

THE HOURS ARE A COMPLETE BLUR of broken memories, out of order, improperly sequenced, totally fucked-up events. I was twelve and had just drunk my first beer—well, more than one. I had blacked out from all the beer I drank, and the next clear thing I can remember is being outside on a hill, completely naked, with this Lee man on top of me trying to shove his penis into my small, unwilling vagina. It was like passing out at point B and fast-forwarding to, say, whatever comes *after* point Z.

He kept saying, "I can't get it in," and I remember asking, as if this was suddenly important, "Am I still a virgin?" The next thing I remember is pushing him off me and running naked to the car, which was parked up on the hill. At the time, it seemed about a thousand miles away. Along the way, I could see all the lights down below and wasn't sure where the hell I was or what time it was or what had just happened or where anybody else was or why we were here in the first place.

I just knew that I wanted to leave. My head was spinning out of control, and I kept blanking in and out of the world around me. I jumped into the driver's seat and tried to start the car up the way I had watched my father do so many times before. It started and I managed to find the lights. I had never driven, and I didn't know where the hell I was going. The car had a stick shift, and I had no idea what to do with this huge thing that had just sprung to life in my hands.

I began jiggling the stick shift fiercely but nothing happened. Nothing, that is, but a lot of horrible sounds from the engine. I was still naked and scared and didn't know what was going on. I didn't know how I got there, and a million questions pulsed through my aching head, the top three being: 1. Where did the preceding hours go? 2. Why was I naked? 3. Where the fuck *was* I?

Instead of answers, suddenly Lisa, her boyfriend, and Lee were running to the car, and then everything went black again.

MY FATHER USED TO TELL ME ALL THE TIME that Skate Escape roller rink, which was in Windgap, Pennsylvania, about 15 miles away from my family's new house, was a "bad place." If I kept going there, he warned that "something bad" would likely happen to me. It was cryptic, but he had this way of predicting the future, and it always pissed me off, because nine times out of ten he was actually right. He always said this to me, but of course when I asked to go, he always gave in and let me, even though in his gut he must have been screaming *not* to let me go. I wish back then he would have listened to his own intuition and not let me do everything I wanted when I wanted to do it.

I was twelve and had been going to the skating rink for a while, hanging with the older kids every weekend. One girl in particular, Lisa, was sixteen; she had become one of my closest friends there. We spoke on the phone all the time and saw each other every weekend. I never thought it was strange that she was so much older than I was and that while she had a car, I hadn't even gotten my period yet.

We got along very well. I was always way beyond my years and usually had trouble relating to people my own age. I'm not sure why this is; maybe I was born an old soul as some would tell me later in life. Anyway, I always felt ten years older than I was. When I think back now, twelve is such a young, tender age, but at the time I felt so old, so mature, so over Barbie dolls and braids.

On this particular weekend, Lisa called to see if I would like to go skating with her, her boyfriend, and his friend. I knew her boyfriend was much older, like in his twenties, and I was nervous about this but also excited. I had never met her boyfriend or his friends. I felt an anxiety in the pit of my stomach that I had never experienced. It engulfed me, and I could barely speak. It was like a wave through my entire body of excitement and fear that was indescribable. I knew my parents wouldn't let me go if I told the truth, so I did what many kids do and do well: I lied to my parents for the first time.

I began begging my parents early in the day. My mother and I had gone to the hairdresser earlier to get haircuts, and I was driving her crazy the whole time. I kept telling her what a great person Lisa was and that she would just be picking me up and taking me to the rink and then bringing me home at 10:00 that night.

All the while I was making sure to complain loudly enough to get the attention of my mother's stylist so she would agree with me and help me convince my mother to let me go. I had learned by this point—or perhaps kids are just born with this ability—that the best way to make your parents cave in is by nagging one of them to the brink of insanity until eventually that parent shoves the responsibility onto the other parent. Instinctively I knew if I could get my mother to say yes or at least, "Ask your father," I was in.

Mom was the gatekeeper. Once I got past her, my father was easy. After all, I was his "baby girl" and he rarely said no to me. All I had to do was crawl up on his lap, flash my baby blues his way, and ask in my sweetest voice, "Please?" He would melt and that would be the end of that. So I knew as long as my mother said those magic words, "I don't care as long as your father says yes," I was as good as gone.

By the time I was done with her at the salon, she cracked and said yes. I went home with victory in hand. I immediately called Lisa and told her I was "almost there" and would call her back after I spoke with my father. I then proceeded to work on him and, after not too much of an argument, he too said yes.

Times were different in the mid-1980s. We didn't have Internet predators. We didn't hear about child abuse and sexual predators as commonly as we do today. There was still a general false sense of safety that surrounded communities, especially suburban communities. So while I look back on this today and wonder how the hell they let me go with total strangers that they had never met, I have to remember that things were different then.

I ARRANGED TO HAVE LISA MEET ME at the entrance to our neighborhood, far away from my actual house. When my parents raised a collective eyebrow, I told them that this was so she wouldn't get lost finding our house. The house was a bit hard to find, and I knew she was coming with her boyfriend and his friend Lee, so I could not let my parents see guys in the car.

I vividly remember my parents not giving me any resistance on this issue, and as I kissed them both good night and walked out the door, I knew deep down something was…strange. I felt weird in the pit of my stomach, all queasy and sick-like. The closer I got to the entrance of my neighborhood, the more I wanted to turn back, run home, and jump into my daddy's lap, but something compelled me to go, and to this day I still don't know what that was…or why.

When I reached the entrance, the car was already waiting for me. Lisa's boyfriend was driving and she was in the front seat. She opened the door, and I climbed into the backseat to find an older man sitting there next to a cooler. He wasn't the boy I envisioned seeing. He was older and looked very rugged and mature. (I would find out later that he was, in fact, twenty-eight years old.) I had taken special care getting ready that night because I had no idea what to expect. I pulled on my yellow rugby shirt with "Swatch" in bold red lettering across the chest and my dark blue Levi's jeans with the thick seam down the middle that curved around to the back of my calf.

With my makeup and hair done to perfection, my body just south of ripeness, I probably looked about fifteen, which is the age Lisa told the man in the backseat. I went along with the lie (fifteen?!) and never asked how old he was. I just assumed he was around eighteen. It seemed so old to me, but whatever. We were just going skating and, as I told myself, nothing major was going to happen.

AFTER DRIVING ABOUT TEN MILES, we turned off way before the skating rink. When I inquired where we were going, they said we were going to go hang out and drink a little before we went skating. "Sure," I remember thinking to myself, "Cool, whatever." I was exhilarated and scared at the same time. Except for the occasional sips I stole from the grasshoppers my mother drank on the holidays, I had never really drunk alcohol before.

We stopped at a clearing by a river and got out of the car. Lee grabbed the cooler with confidence and brought it outside with us. I followed Lisa over to a large rock, where we both sat down. The guys dropped down beside us, each with two sixteen-ounce Busch "pounders" in their hands. Just like that, Lee handed me a beer. No drum roll, no diploma. Do not pass go, just go straight to adulthood.

I had never held a beer in my life, let alone this big, long can that I could barely fit my twelve-year-old hand around. (Did Lee notice? Or just not care?) I remember how cold it felt and the moisture dripping down the side glistening in a very inviting way. I just looked at it for a while and watched as the others began to drink. Finally, I tilted the can to my mouth and felt the cold rush of foam and bitter liquid as it hit my tongue and streamed down my throat.

I just kept tilting the can back, farther and farther. I enjoyed the almost immediate rush that went through my temples and up to the top of my scalp. Instantly, my head began to feel light, and it was hard to focus. I loved this feeling. It was immediate and all right with me. I was giddy and began laughing—at nothing at all—for no reason at all. No one noticed or, if they noticed, cared. I had slipped, unseen and undiscovered, into the land of adults.

If I didn't exactly belong there, I must not have stood out too much, either. We were all just hanging out and talking, drinking, and laughing. It felt very harmless, and

I was thirsty, more thirsty than I could ever remember being before. I kept drinking one tallboy after another until I had to pee so badly I couldn't hold it anymore. I told Lisa, and she was like, "Well, we're going to have to go in the bushes since there are no bathrooms."

Yippee! Another rite of passage. This was my first outdoor urination, and I was laughing the whole time as we both pulled our pants down and almost fell on top of each other. I never had to pee so badly in all my life. When it finally came and began to flow between my legs onto the ground, I felt a release that was amazing, better than anything I had ever felt. Like a current, it sent electricity through my body as the little puddle began to splash up onto my shoe. I thought that was very gross, and we both just laughed about it.

Between giggling bouts, Lisa joked about how Lee liked me and asked if I thought he was cute. I was snorting, my head was spinning, and I couldn't really form a complete thought, but I told her, "I think he's cute, I guess." We went back to where the guys were sitting, and it was clear from the way they zipped it that they had been discussing the same thing. We sat there for a long time just drinking and talking, talking and drinking. I don't remember about what, exactly; I just remember I kept drinking and it began to get dark.

The last thing I remember consciously thinking was, "Are we ever going roller-skating?"

THE CAR DOOR OPENED AND I WAS LEANING OUT from the backseat into the brisk cold air to vomit. Nasty bile kept exploding out of my throat and I couldn't stop it. It burned so badly I thought blood would surely follow. I was finally able to stop vomiting long enough for Lisa to shut the door. I don't know how I got in the backseat of the car, but we were in motion, driving away from the hill, and I was now fully dressed. The last thing I remembered was trying to wiggle the stick shift to get away. We had driven back into town and were pulling in to the bowling alley next to Skate Escape. The guys were being quiet and seemed pissed off, and Lisa dragged me into the bathroom asking me, of all things, what the hell my problem was.

I was confused. I had no idea what time it was or what had happened. What the hell was wrong with me? I got into the bathroom just in time to slam into the door of the stall and (big surprise) vomit some more. I felt horrible, my head was throbbing, I was dirty all over, and from between my legs came an odd, dull throbbing.

As I stood up to clean my mouth, I noticed my reflection in the mirror. I looked totally different: older, worse, and scarier than I could ever have imagined looking before. My hair was a mess, I had dirt on my clothes and my face, and there were these big red-purplish bruises on my neck. Lisa saw me inspecting these with a questioning look and said, "Those are hickeys, Jen. Haven't you ever had a hickey before?"

I looked at her in a confused daze and said nothing. I just wanted to go home, but I was petrified. I didn't understand what the last couple of hours consisted of and where I would be going next. I kept silent because I could tell Lisa was mad at me. Why? I kept wondering what I had done wrong. What did I miss?

Instead of asking, I remained silent in the hopes that I would not piss them off any further.

LISA'S BOYFRIEND DECIDED WE WOULD GO BACK to his house and crash. I didn't want to go but couldn't get myself to say anything to the contrary; suddenly my throat was paralyzed. We went back to his house and went into his room. Lisa and her boyfriend climbed into bed and turned off the lights and left me and Lee on the floor. I just sat there, not sure what to do, and Lee kept asking me what was wrong. After about five minutes, I heard strange noises coming from above and realized with absolute certainty (although I had no basis for comparison) that Lisa and her boyfriend were having sex.

This was the first time I had heard people having sex. Lee wanted me to lie down with him. I tried to for a moment but when he put his arm around me, I felt the bile in my throat rise again. My whole body stiffened, and I wanted to scream but I couldn't. Instead I asked where the bathroom was and he told me. I stumbled through the apartment looking for a phone. I still had no idea what time it was, but I knew it was late and my parents would be worried sick. I was scared to call, but I picked up the phone anyway and dialed my number.

I don't remember how long it rang, but knowing my parents, it couldn't have been long. A frantic voice answered, and I recognized my mother. Her voice was trembling as she asked me where I was. I said I didn't know but I would be home as soon as possible and that I was sorry. She began asking all these questions: "Where are you? Who are you with? Where have you been?"

I hung up in fear, mostly because I didn't know the answers to her questions. I then proceeded back to the bedroom and loudly announced that I needed to go home immediately, that I had just called my parents and they were very worried and wanted me home. I heard Lisa's boyfriend grumbling from the bed, and they both began to fumble for their clothes.

THEY DROVE ME HOME IN TOTAL SILENCE. When we pulled up to my house, we saw police cars in the driveway. Lisa's boyfriend turned to me and said, "Nothing happened, okay? You are okay, right?" I just looked at him, shocked, amazed, and stupefied, but no more shocked, amazed, and stupefied than I'd been for the last God knows how many hours. I was far from fucking okay, but I couldn't say that. I just stared at him with a blankness that I had never felt before.

Lisa said, "It's okay, Jen. Just tell them you were at the skating rink and we lost track of time." Lee was in the backseat, silent and looking at the splatters of my puke still on his shoes. I got out of the car and slowly began to walk up to my house. It seemed like hours before I actually made it to the front door. As I turned the knob, like I had done so many times before, I knew my life was about to change forever.

3

Being Judged

MY HEAD WAS SPINNING and I had never been so scared, ashamed, and horrified in my life. I walked in and saw my father sitting on a kitchen stool looking much older than I remembered. A police officer was standing by our kitchen sink, and another one was behind my father. My mother came running over to me. Behind my father, I could see my brothers coming out of their room. As my mother approached me, her face changed very quickly from one of concern to one of utter disgust, and she slapped my face so hard I instantly began to cry.

I knew she had seen the bruises on my neck, and I didn't know how to explain them. I was filled with so much fear from seeing the look in her eyes that I could not stop weeping. Her expression changed once again to one of instant understanding and fear. She took my hand and led me into the bathroom, where she quietly asked me to remove my clothing. Just like that: "Remove your clothing." So formal.

I began taking my Levi's off and pulled my underwear down to my ankles. They were covered in dirt and a little blood lay at the bottom of them. My mother looked down and then up at me and began to sob with me. Her expression changed again, and I think she finally realized that something very bad had happened, something I hadn't brought on myself, something I couldn't have controlled.

My body was shaking uncontrollably and I had never felt so utterly, completely, uncontrollably *ashamed*. I wished at that moment that I were invisible. She told me to put my clothes back on and walked me back to the kitchen, where the police, my father, and both my brothers—five grown (or nearly grown) men—were waiting to find out what was going on. My mother said in a low, quivering voice, "We need to take her to the hospital. I think she was assaulted."

HOURS LATER, AND A WORLD APART, I walked through my front door as I had a million times before, but this time it was different. Not it. *I* was different, older somehow, numb and tired. I had just spent Easter morning in metal stirrups with some doctor who looked like Tony Orlando, and with a rape-victim advocate holding one hand and my mother holding the other.

I kept asking if I would still be able to have children. For some reason, something in my head told me that this abuse had robbed me of the ability to bear children. (As if I wasn't still a child myself.) I'm not sure where this idea came from; maybe it was because I felt so robbed and empty and I needed to explain the loss I felt. They informed me that because I was so little physically, Lee had not fully penetrated me nor did he break my hymen. So technically I was still a virgin. "Great," I thought, "whatever that really means."

AS I ENTERED THE VERY KITCHEN I had stood in just hours before, I saw my brothers standing in the dining room, looking back as if they didn't quite know how to react to me. My father picked up the phone as it rang and walked into the other room with it. I heard him telling whoever was on the other end that I had been raped, at which point he burst into tears, sobbing as he held the phone. This was the first time I had ever heard my father cry. I knew something huge had happened and that things in our family would never be the same, all because I selfishly wanted to go out on my own that night.

My brother Brian ran into his room, jumped onto his top bunk, and began to sob into his pillow. I just stood there, numb as could be, as the walls of my secure, happy family began to fall down all around me, and I was left alone in the middle to blame. At least this is what I thought for years and years to come.

Well, what else *could* I think?

AFTER THAT DAY WE NEVER REALLY SPOKE about what had happened. No one ever told me I wasn't to blame; they just looked at me strangely. No one held me and said, "It's okay to cry, baby; it will all be okay." No one ever told me that the noises at night were just our house creaking and not that man coming to get me. No one ever said, "Jennifer, that is *not* what sex is; *this* is what it is."

No one ever said that.

No one ever said anything. Meanwhile, I interpreted their silence as meaning they thought the attempted rape was my fault. I was dirty and we don't speak of these things. I was bad and not worthy of consoling.

I told my best friend what had happened, and she thought I was dirty, too, because the next day she passed a note to everyone in the cafeteria saying that I was a slut and that I deserved it.

I must have been bad. No one wanted to talk to me about it, and everyone blamed me.

LEE HAD BEEN CHARGED with several counts, including rape, statutory rape, deviant sexual intercourse, indecent assault, indecent exposure, and corruption of a minor. The deviant sexual intercourse was dropped right away because he had not attempted to orally or anally penetrate me. A preliminary hearing date was set, and I was prepared by the district attorney's office to testify. I didn't have a victim advocate with me that day that I recall.

Weeks later, I was sitting on the witness stand, shaking and giddy, unable to control anything around me; my emotions were swinging from absolute fear to uncontrollable laughter. This was no laughing matter, but I felt like I was about to lose it, sitting in this wooden box with a judge on my right and the man who inserted himself into my life across from me looking so smug in his old, worn-out, red hooded sweatshirt and jeans that he wore for this judgment day—no coat, no collared shirt, no tie for *his* day in court.

I had to relive that strange night that only came to me in bits and pieces and that I really didn't ever want to recall, as my lawyer gently tried to pull details from my absent mind. I wasn't really there. I heard noises all around me: the quiet consultation of this man and his lawyer and the questions my lawyer asked. I sensed my parents' dull silence, but I was above it all as though floating in a protective bubble. Above the pain, above the noise, above the man who in a few short hours took my innocence, my parents' little girl.

Maybe if I stayed up here long enough, I thought, it would all pass by like storm clouds on a hot, humid summer day just before the rain stops and the rainbow peeks out. I could find a clearing and swim safely in a beautiful blue abyss. But I quickly snapped back to reality by the judge, who asked me if I found this process amusing, and I didn't know how to respond because I wasn't aware I was laughing.

I stared blankly from him past the man in the red hooded sweatshirt to the pained, horrified looks on my parents' faces until I heard my lawyer apologizing and reassuring the judge that it's normal for someone my age to get giddy in stressful situations. I think that was where I learned to use humor as a defense; it's so much easier to laugh instead of screaming or crying, easier to laugh at yourself before someone laughs at you.

I DON'T REMEMBER LEAVING THE COURTROOM, just that it was over, and a couple of months later I overheard my parents saying that he was sentenced to two years in jail. I was angry at them for not telling me when the sentencing was so I could go and maybe, just maybe, find some closure for myself. They apologized; they said they wanted to protect me and didn't really think I needed to go. That was them, though, always thinking for me but never telling me about any of it and panicking if I actually discovered it.

4

Normal, Relatively

I WAS BORN IN WILSON, PENNSYLVANIA, right outside
the Jersey border, in a little townhouse. For the first
fifteen years of my life, I thought I had been born
on the kitchen table. Many times my two older brothers
would remind me of this and then laugh when I eagerly
told my friends this dramatic story of my birth.

The true story, of course, wasn't as dramatic but
certainly was unusual. My mother was lying in bed one
night and began having contractions; my father was home
and our neighbors had come over. Both of my brothers
were in the room when my mother began to cry out in
unexpected and unbearable pain. No one knew what to do.
My mother wasn't due to have me for another two weeks,
and my father began to panic. He called 911 and my aunt,
who lived nearby. My aunt arrived first, and my parents'
small bedroom began to clutter up with people and chaos
as I began to make myself into the world. Within a very
short time after contractions started, I quickly slipped out
of my mother's body and onto the very bed sheets where
my conception had taken place.

My aunt helped deliver me about the same time that
firefighters and ambulance technicians arrived. The

room was filled with people as I came into the world with as much drama as I would grow accustomed to over the next twenty years, with all eyes on me, making a fucking mess. My father said there was more blood than he had ever seen, and my brother Jimmy, who watched the whole thing, thought my mother and I were dying.

I was only briefly placed into my mother's arms, then put into an incubator under observation as any infant is when it is born in an unusual manner. My mother later told me that I had almost died. I fought the odds and lived. In some way I see this as the beginning of my personal fight for survival.

LOOKING AT THE FEW PICTURES THAT EXIST from my childhood—for whatever reason, the baby books significantly dwindled by the time it came to capture my precious moments—and blushing over the shag carpet or pageboy haircuts, I vividly remember not really ever fitting in or feeling...*whole*. There are no pictures of me with my mother in the hospital at all. An instant mother-daughter connection was not made on my birth day, and for the next twenty-two years I struggled with trying to obtain that connection with her, that wonderful camaraderie all my friends seemed to have with their mothers. Or the wonderfully idealistic relationship that Laura Ingalls Wilder seemed to have with her mother in the *Little House on the Prairie* books I loved so much, that tender love and affection. I longed for unconditional love and support, and when I couldn't find them in my own house, I read about the lives of others. In my head I became them—and for hours upon hours I would get lost in the pages of *Sweet Valley High* novels, in which a huge crisis always changed the lives of all the characters but in the end worked out in some amazing way.

I used to read a lot, a book a day sometimes. That seemed to help. I remember our brown leather kitchen chairs had wheels on them. I would curl up in one and sit by the window all day spinning around in circles and losing myself in the pages. I would become the characters in the books. I traveled through time and saw life through the eyes of these colorful characters. I could not get enough. I would read as fast as I could, boring myself deeper and deeper into the ink on the pages that soon became my reality. My only reality.

My existence in that very moment was whatever path the author took me down. Some days it was down the yellow brick road, others it was into outer space. Some days I was in the Deep South, others I was in the deepest jungle. Those crisp pages were my solitude, my fantasy, and I got lost in them in a way that made me never want to find my way back to reality. As much as I looked forward to beginning a new book, I dreaded its ending. By then the characters had become friends and the author my mentor, and when they deserted me on the final page, I felt betrayed and abandoned. I truly believed I was living the events I was reading. At the time, it was the only truth I knew.

I loved going to our local bookstore and just being around books, something about being in the midst of a million different escape routes brought me a great sense of relief.

TO THIS DAY I AM UNCERTAIN what I was trying to escape from then, because early on it would seem that my life was normal. I had two parents who were married, and at the time, I believed they loved each other very much. Early in my childhood, my parents seemed to have a nice life; they would go out to dinner or parties with my aunt and uncle or with their friends and always had love in their eyes for one another. My dad went to work, and my mother took care of the house.

My parents always told my brothers and me that they would never break up, like so many of our friends' parents had done over the years. They always assured us that would never happen. We always knew we were loved, probably too much at times. By that, I mean we were spoiled, especially at Christmastime. My parents went nuts over Christmas, and I do mean nuts. Every year, we each received at least thirty presents, which were to be opened in a ritual, in a specific order my parents had predetermined. It didn't matter where we were living at the time or how well my dad was doing financially, we always had a *huge* Christmas.

We moved several times as my father went through many jobs. Let's see, we went from Wilson, Pennsylvania, where I was born, to Nazareth, Pennsylvania, when I was three. Then we went to Franklin, Tennessee, for a year when I was nine, then back to Pennsylvania to a little town called Bath for a year. And then we moved to a trailer park called Hickory Hills in Moore Township, Pennsylvania, where we stayed until I was seventeen. Ah, stability! Ha.

At some point through all the moves, my mother became incredibly unhappy. As my father struggled to raise us all and find his niche in the workforce, she drifted away. She had never wanted to move out of our house in Nazareth; to be honest, neither did the rest of us. But my father had this great opportunity to make much more money in Tennessee, and he would be able to provide us with a better life, so we moved into a beautiful mansion in a gated community. The neighborhood was so big that the first time I rode my bike I got lost and had to have a neighbor take me home. However, my father's business didn't do well at all.

During all these moves, I watched my parents' relationship slowly fall apart. I saw my mother change and become this lifeless, bitter, resentful person who yelled at my father and us kids all the time. Nothing any of us did, including my dad, was right; she always had something negative to say about everything and everybody. I don't know what happened or when, but a part of my mother died at some point during those twenty-five years of marriage. Or maybe I do know and harbored the blame myself for years. Maybe it was the day I was born, the day another "woman" came into my father's life. My mom could not stand sharing the spotlight. She had been my dad's princess for so long, and he was her knight in shining armor; he had rescued her from her alcoholic mother and abusive stepfather at age sixteen. My dad had been both her lover and a father figure, and when I was born, she resented his love for me, because in her twisted mind she thought it meant he loved her less. At least that's what I thought. I paid for this belief emotionally.

AFTER MY BIRTH, MY MOTHER began taking Valium because of the traumatic nature of my delivery—or at least that was her excuse. Throughout my childhood I vividly remember being reminded that she had to take these pills because her nerves were so strained from my birth. I often wondered why ten and even fifteen years later she was still taking them; I must have still been affecting her nerves. Maybe my very presence reminded her of the horror of that night and she couldn't conceive of life without the gentle release those pretty yellow pills gave her. I often opened her pill bottle when she wasn't looking and watched these pills spill out into my hand. Even then I sensed that they had great power. I swished them around in my hand, taking my little finger and outlining the V that was imprinted in the center. I hated these pills, yet was totally fascinated by them. There was something about their very existence that made me feel small and, in many ways, bad. My mommy had to take these pills in order to deal with life because of me.

My relationship with my mother was always all or nothing; I was either totally subservient to her or totally absent. I remember around Christmastime my mother would get very depressed and cry a lot, and I had no idea why or what to do. This started when we moved to Tennessee. After that, it just became a known fact in our house that Mommy got sad at Christmastime because of her dad, but I never really understood the why of it all. The first time it happened, she went into the dining room of our beautiful house in Tennessee and cried in the dark, and I walked in, put my arms around her waist, and told her it was okay and that I loved her.

My mother's father had disowned her a long time ago, before we moved to Tennessee; it was sometime when I was around three or four, and to this day I still have no clear idea why. I do remember him. When I was very small, we would visit him and his new wife in New Jersey. I remember sitting on his lap and the love he gave me and the wonderful presents they had for us and the candy all around their house, jars filled with those shiny candies that look like the ribbons on presents. I loved those ribbon candies. Funny how grandparents always have candy. Is there something in old age that makes you crave sugar? Is it the lack of sex? Is it knowing that you don't have much time left, so you can indulge? I always found this obsession with sweets amazing.

Anyway, one day we stopped going there, and after that my mother often cried, especially around holidays. My parents never really explained. Come to think of it, my parents never really explained much of anything when it came to family and feelings, anything other than factual information.

ON MY MOTHER'S SIDE, I had lots of cousins, aunts, and uncles whom I never really saw, maybe only a handful of times in my life, because my father said they were "trash." They were all "drug addicts and alcoholics," and we were told repeatedly that he would not subject his children to that kind of lifestyle. The exception to this was my alcoholic grandmother, my mom's mother, who lived with us on and off my entire life. We grew up knowing my parents' closest friends as our aunts and uncles and their children as our cousins.

My favorite "uncle" was my dad's best friend John. I loved going over to his big house for picnics and holidays. John came from a huge Italian family. I loved being around all of them, because it gave me some semblance of what it was like to have normal extended family.

Uncle John was a warm-hearted man who always made me smile and feel loved. If I was sad, he would put me on his lap and sing this funny song that, no matter how upset or angry I was, always melted me into a puddle of giggles. He would sing lyrics to "Shaddup You Face" by Joe Dolce in his thick Italian dialect. Still to this day, when I get upset, I will hear my Uncle John's voice in my head singing that song, and it puts a smile on my face. It is one of those warm-fuzzy memories that, unfortunately, I have few of, so I cherish it like a baby blanket.

MY FAMILY USED HUMOR to deal with everything, which always made for a lot of laughter in my house. I grew up learning how to make a joke out of anything. My father was not good at expressing himself verbally, so instead he would just make a humorous comment to break the tension and ease his own anxiety. It came in handy for me as a coping mechanism throughout my life. My father knew two emotions, happy and angry, and he expressed them well. He didn't get angry often—in fact it took a lot to piss him off—but once he did, look out.

I was close with my two older brothers and looked up to them so much. They picked on me all the time and played mean little jokes on me, just like many older brothers do. And no matter how much I was hurt or humiliated, I always went back for more.

At night when I was scared and couldn't sleep, I would creep into their room and ask if I could sleep with them. They always said yes, but I had to sleep at the bottom of the bed because there was not enough room at the top. I'd curl up into a ball at their feet. As soon as I felt secure and safe, I'd drift off to sleep, and naturally it was always at this time that my brothers would straighten their feet and with a swift kick launch me right off the bed onto the hard floor. Feeling the hurt of my bruised body, I would pick myself up and try to run into my room as soon as I could, because surely my father had heard the loud thump and would come running up the stairs to find out what the noise was and why we were still awake.

I always got busted running back into my bed and got yelled at, while my brothers stifled their laughter. Even so, as my father went back downstairs yelling, "If I have to come up here one more time...," I'd creep back into my brothers' room and ask if I could sleep with them again. I knew I'd get yelled at or worse, depending on the mood my father was in that night. We never got seriously hit or anything, but if we pissed him off on the wrong night, his brown leather belt would come out and go straight across our bare asses. The welts would remain for hours. I feared making my father angry because of that belt, and if I knew it was coming, I began to cry and scream out, in hopes that he would feel bad and not do it, and also to prepare myself for the pain I was about to endure.

I WAS ALWAYS A GLUTTON FOR PUNISHMENT; it never failed that even when I got in trouble I went back for more. Foreseeing bad consequences never stopped me from doing things; it usually had the opposite effect. From early childhood, the idea of getting into trouble or getting caught excited me to some degree. The challenge of getting away with something or doing something "bad" gave me such an adrenaline rush! I craved that tingling sensation in my stomach and the absolute excitement that would soar through my body like an electric jolt at the moment I knew with certainty that I could get caught for doing something I wasn't supposed to do.

This fascination with being "bad" stayed with me for a long time, and as I got older the consequences just kept getting worse. I also had an amazing sense of invincibility—thinking nothing could hurt me or stop me from doing what I wanted. Plus, I always thought things would be different, that no matter how many times I went into my brothers' room and got kicked off the bed, at some point they would not kick me off. But it never changed.

It was like Charlie Brown with Lucy and the football; no matter how many times she pulled it away, he always went back for more, one more time, always believing she wouldn't betray him, couldn't possibly betray him. I would go into my brothers' room, they would let me lie down, I would start to fall asleep, then they would kick me off and my father would come running and I would be the one to get in trouble. Nothing was ever different other than that my father would be angrier each time he had to come up the stairs, and the consequences for me worsened with each transgression.

I believe they call this the definition of insanity: doing the same thing over and over again and expecting a different result. I definitely believe that people are born with a predisposition to addiction, and with my family history, it was no wonder I was exhibiting classic signs of addictive behavior at such an early age. After all, in active addiction, insanity reigns supreme. If that's the case, then I was insane for a very long time. I never learned from any of my mistakes. I had this inborn sense that I could overcome the impossible without changing anything about my part in the situation. This belief would eventually get me into severe trouble, but at the time it seemed quite innocent.

I REMEMBER TAKING MY FIRST SIP of an alcoholic drink at around six or seven years old. My parents would have gatherings at the house and invite their friends. I was not supposed to be out of my bedroom, but I would sometimes come downstairs in my little pajamas and walk around. At the time my mother was always drinking light green drinks in small glasses, and I loved the color of the drink. It was the same color as my bedroom walls and the plastic lights on my nightstand. I was drawn to the color, and when no one was looking, I picked up the glass and took a little taste. It tasted like mint, sweet and slightly bitter, and my tongue tingled and woke up. I loved it immediately and took a bigger sip before running back upstairs. I got a little head rush as I landed on my bed; it was subtle but mixed the alcohol with the adrenaline of being downstairs and doing something I shouldn't have been doing. It was exhilarating. After that, my favorite ice cream flavor was mint chocolate chip.

I remember one day my mother stayed all day in her long, bright orange nightgown drinking coffee at the kitchen table, and in my mind she stayed like this for years. In some ways, she never left that table, or that nightgown, or that mood. Moping around the house with soap operas on the TV, she would occasionally do the laundry or run the vacuum, but for the most part she just sat at the kitchen table drinking coffee and smoking cigarettes with her mother, my grandmother. The only difference between them was that my grandmother always had a can of beer instead of coffee in her hand. I would study these women, the role models set before me, and wonder if this was what I was going to do when I grew up.

I found it ironic that my father sheltered us from our cousins, aunts, and uncles because they were all drunks and addicts, but he allowed my grandmother, who was an alcoholic, to live under our very roof and drink daily at our kitchen table. She and my mother would sit around and bitch about the neighbors or members of our family who were not living up to the right standards or my father, who wasn't making enough money for them to spend.

It made me never want to be home. The negative energy in our home was palpable. I wanted nothing more than to be away from home all the time at this point. I was young, but old enough to ride. Ride my bike, my skateboard, later my roller skates. Anything and everything that had wheels became my vehicle away from that kitchen table, those soap operas, the constant wafting of smoke and discontent. I rode and rode, and when I could ride no more, I'd turn around and ride back. The longer I stayed away from home, the less I was missed. The less I was missed, the better I felt. The better I felt, the longer I stayed away from home, and the less...well, you get the picture. If only staying away from home hadn't been like leaping out of the frying pan into the fire.

5

Valentines and Dirty Dancing

ONE YEAR, WHEN WE WERE LIVING in a townhouse in Bath, my oldest brother Jimmy had his birthday party at an old roller rink in Easton. This is where I first put on a pair of skates and learned how to slide across the wooden floor with the rest of the teens in the eighties.

At first I clung to the wall for dear life as others flew by me, crossing their skates at every turn as if their legs and the wheels were one. I was totally in awe of this movement. I wanted to learn how to gracefully slide across the floor, how to grip the corners of the rink and dance while I coasted through the swarms of brightly dressed, gaily laughing people. Instead, I clung to the railing like a beached whale, following the movements of the other skaters and waiting for the right time to make my move—like those girls who do those jump rope tricks on the sidewalk in summer.

I eventually left the wall and braved the middle of the rink, tottering on wobbly, coltish legs, like those newborn foals you see on *Animal Planet* or the Discovery Channel. You had to give me credit; slowly I began to slide one foot in front of the other, and in the youthful agility that sometimes contradicts the awkwardness of adolescence, I was soon gliding like a swan.

I loved being able to glide so freely, unencumbered by gravity, by the cares of my normal world. After that day, I began to live on roller skates. I skated around the house all the time. I can't describe the freedom I felt propped upon those eight little wheels. I had found an escape and I loved it. When we moved from the townhouse in Bath to a trailer park about seven miles away, I began to start going to a local roller rink often. Appropriately, the roller rink was named Skate Escape, this little place on top of a huge hill in Windgap.

I STARTED GOING TO SKATE ESCAPE every weekend when I was about eleven years old. My parents let me go during the day, and eventually, after much begging and pleading, they let me go on Friday and Saturday nights, too. I look back on it now and can't believe that I was only eleven when I started going there. I can't imagine letting an eleven-year-old go anywhere by herself at night these days, yet back then it was more common to drop your children off and pick them up hours later. The world was a different place then.

My friend Kristen and I would get all dressed up in the latest fashions and head off to Skate Escape. At this time roller rinks were the shit; they were *the* place to be. The regulars were there every weekend, and if you wanted to be anything more than a fly on the wall, they were the people to get to know and be friends with. Kristen and I quickly started to hang out with all the right people; we flirted with the DJ and got in good with the boy who worked the shoe rental.

Skate Escape was a little rink. You walked through the first set of doors to a window where you would pay and get your tickets to go inside. The next set of double doors opened up to the skating rink proper. A concession stand was on the right with about six tables and booths. On the left was where you got your skates—that is, if you weren't cool enough to own your own pair. The rental skates were these ugly greenish-brown things with orange laces and brown wheels, definitely not the shit.

Naturally, I begged my parents for months to buy me a pair of my own. Eventually they gave in and bought me a beautiful pair of white skates with blue wheels. I loved those skates. Not only did they look ultra-cool, but they meant I didn't have to stand in the stupid line and put on those ugly skates every weekend. They meant I had a chance to become one of the cool regulars I looked up to.

THERE WAS ONE GIRL I was totally infatuated with; she wore tons of makeup and her hair was done up in huge curls using about half a can of Aqua Net. I thought she looked just like one of those girls in the Prince videos that were so popular on MTV at the time. I wanted to be her. I began to wear lots of colors on my face—purple eye shadow, pink mascara, big red lips—the tackiest mix of colors you can imagine.

It was the eighties and everything was extreme and big: big shiny belts hanging off the tightest of spandex pants; big, colorful printed shirts with shoulder pads that made the tiniest little girl look like a linebacker for the Rams. The hair was big—the bigger the better. I remember my hair being very long, and I would take a pick and some Aqua Net hairspray to it for over an hour until it was so high off my head I would hit doorways when entering.

My father called this look "mall hair." Even ninety-mile-per-hour winds were no competition for this particular hairstyle. I can say that to this day I am so grateful the look has yet to come back into style. Looking back, I see it was brutal, but at the time I loved it and thought I was the shit. Week after week I primped and prepared and went back to the roller rink, eventually making all the right friends and connections.

I had lots of friends and several boyfriends during this time. I was only eleven years old, so when I say "boyfriend," I mean a boy I had a crush on but never actually did anything with. You know, like the type of boyfriend you have when you are a little girl. Totally innocent.

Then again, some of my habits weren't so innocent. I began smoking during this time. Everyone at the rink smoked Marlboro Lights. Why not? There was a cigarette machine in the concession area, and I found myself puffing on my friends' cigarettes often. They tasted terrible, but everyone looked so cool smoking that I just sucked it up and smoked them anyway. My parents were smokers, and it was common for me and my clothes to smell like smoke anyway, so I easily got away with it.

I WAS SPENDING ALL MY TIME with my friend Kristen, who had thin brown hair that went all the way down her back and was cut real short on the sides and top. Commonly referred to as a mullet these days, it was cool and in style back in the eighties, though scary and not so cool today.

Sometimes I would cut Kristen's hair. I liked the way it felt right after it had been washed. I would pretend to be this great hairstylist and section pieces of her soft, wet hair as I took the scissors and imitated what I had seen stylists do at the beauty shop. Then I would blow-dry each section very carefully and style it with lots of mousse and hairspray until it was as big as I could get it.

Blackout Girl

Kristen always liked it when I did her hair, and she often encouraged me to become a stylist for real. I always dismissed the idea, because I did not want to have to stand all day and touch nasty people's hair. I liked doing hers because I liked her, but I didn't think I would like to play with a stranger's hair.

Kristen was a year older than me but in my grade at school; she was held back a year because her parents thought she needed "some extra time to learn." She was my best friend and, as best friends do, we told each other *everything*. She lived two doors down from me in the trailer park, so we slept at each other's houses every chance we could get. If we weren't at each other's houses, then we were on the phone constantly. Our parents complained about our incessant need to be with each other every day.

I would go with Kristen and her parents on Friday nights to Bible study at her parents' friends' house. They were born-again Christians and very strict about religion and God. Kristen's mother was a very large, warm person with white hair and a big smile. Kristen's stepfather was about twenty years older than her mother. He was mean and scary; he yelled at us for everything no matter what we did. I don't remember ever seeing him smile. I always wondered why her mother was with him and why she just didn't leave and find someone younger and nicer. I didn't understand why they had all these meetings about the Bible or what they spoke about, but I knew it was something very serious, and when they were having their meetings, we had to be on our best behavior.

When Kristen wasn't looking, I would go into the kitchen cabinet and take down the small round wafers that I had seen her parents use in their studies and place one on my tongue. It felt very dry until I closed my mouth on it. Surrounding the wafer with my saliva, I would immediately feel it stick to the top of my mouth and begin to dissolve. I loved the way it tasted, kind of like an ice cream cone. Whenever Kristen caught me, she would get all scared and yell that if her parents saw me we would be in big trouble. Yet every time I was there, I would always eat one.

I THOUGHT KRISTEN had the most beautiful blue eyes I had ever seen. They looked like rare jewels, and I sometimes just stared into them and swum around while she rattled on and on about the new Madonna album that had just come out or how Patrick Swayze was the hottest boy ever in that new movie *Dirty Dancing*. It didn't matter much what she was saying at those moments, just that she keep talking so I could keep staring.

Kristen and I talked about boys and wondered what it would be like to French kiss one. Sometimes we would practice on our knees, then critique each other. I remember very strongly wanting to practice with Kristen and I think she wanted to as well. We would just look at each other for a while and then, after a very uncomfortable pause, change the subject.

IN KINDERGARTEN, I TOTALLY FELL for this girl named Skye with long blonde hair and blue eyes. I just assumed everyone else felt the way I did about girls. We would sit around in class and play with each other's hair. My hair was long and very thick, and everyone loved playing with it. I loved the way it felt when others touched it; my scalp would get all tingly, and tiny vibrations would run up and down my spine. To this day, I still love it when someone plays with my hair.

AFTER FOURTH GRADE WE MOVED to Tennessee and there were twins in my class. They were beautiful. They fascinated me for two reasons. First, they reminded me of the books I began reading about that time, *Sweet Valley High* and *Sweet Valley Twins*, and second, they were so pretty. I always used to fantasize that I had a twin my parents gave away at birth and that one day she would show up and we would live happily ever after. Garden-variety pop psychology stuff, I know. I guess I was just looking for someone to *get* me, someone to connect with.

It was around Valentine's Day and our teacher, Ms. Jackson, a large, cheery black woman, told us that we should start our list and choose our valentines. I decided that I wanted to make the twins my valentines. Clearly I was already very ambitious in the love department. I started to write these little love notes and signed them all "from your secret admirer." I slipped them into their "mailboxes," which each of us had at the front of the classroom, green hanging folders with our names on them.

I was very sneaky, so no one caught me. Later in the day, when one of them checked her folder, she would see the note and alert the other that she had one, too. It was excitingly voyeuristic, though I didn't know what the word meant back then—or if I could have even pronounced it! I sat across the room and watched them get all excited as they read the notes. Then we all gathered around and giggled about how they both had a "secret admirer." This went on for days, and each day I wrote poems and drew pretty hearts and pictures for each of them. I didn't think there was anything wrong with writing girls love notes. No one had ever told me that it was odd.

One morning as I was slipping a note into one twin's folder, Ms. Jackson caught me. She had a look of horror and confusion on her face as she realized I was the famed "secret admirer." I vividly remember her pulling me aside in the classroom and in a very stern voice telling me that it was *not* okay that I wrote love notes to girls. I was supposed to like boys, and it was not "normal" to like girls. She was very serious, and she scared me with each word that she spoke. She told me she was going to rip up my love letters and not tell a soul that I had written them as long as I stopped my "inappropriate behavior" immediately. My eyes were as wide as saucers as she told me that I wasn't normal and that my feelings weren't okay.

That day on the bus, I sat next to Benji, a cute boy with brown curly hair and big blue eyes. He always told me how pretty I was and that he liked me. That day I let Benji kiss me on the lips. I thought about what Ms. Jackson had said and figured I had better start liking boys soon or people would think I wasn't normal. I didn't really like the kiss, but I went along with it anyway. I figured eventually I would just start to like it.

TWO GRADES IN SCHOOL, TWO CRUSHES, and one boy kiss later, at age eleven I sat talking with Kristen about kissing boys. I never let on that I didn't really want to. I just said it because I thought I was *supposed* to say it. The whole time, all I wanted to do was kiss *her*. My feelings were still there; they hadn't gone away. I knew from her eyes and the weirdness of it all that something was going on, that I was attracted to her in the way that Joanie was to Chachi on *Happy Days*, yet my Chachi had brilliant blue eyes—and breasts. I didn't know what to do about these feelings and wasn't sure I was supposed to be having them, especially after what Ms. Jackson had told me on Valentine's Day two years earlier.

Kristen and I would talk about our feelings sometimes while lying in bed giving each other back massages with hot oil—and no shirts. We both felt an electricity between us and didn't know what it was or what it meant.

One night we were in her bedroom after watching Dirty Dancing, and we were trying to do dances we had seen in the movie. We held each other very tightly, our hips touching gently. My arms were around her neck and hers were around my waist, and we began to grind our bodies up against each other like we had seen the actors do.

Something happened to me. I began to feel all hot and tingly, and my crotch began to burn and become moist. I knew she felt this, too, and without saying anything we continued to dance, pushing ourselves harder up against each other without making eye contact. I thought that if I looked up and saw her blue eyes, she would see the hunger in mine and run away from me, but I began to raise my eyes anyway. I needed to see if she had the same feelings.

AT THAT PRECISE MOMENT her father walked into the room and found us fully dressed, but all wrapped up in each other's arms grinding to the soundtrack of Dirty Dancing. The look on his face was pure disgust, and he began screaming things like "lezzy" and "you're going to hell." I frantically looked around the room for my shoes and my jacket. In my confused state, I somehow found them and ran past him out the door as I heard various biblical passages being screamed at my back.

I ran into the wooded area by our house and collapsed onto the wooden picnic table there, my mind swimming with the events that just happened. My first thought was,

"What the hell is a lezzy and why am I all of a sudden doomed to hell?" I had never seen two women together, or two men for that matter, but I had not known it was so wrong. I suppose my parents didn't raise me to believe that such things even existed, let alone that something that felt so natural and right between two people could be so wrong. I was so confused and at the same time so elated by what I had just experienced. I was scared. What did this all mean? Was Kristen's father going to let me in their home again? Would I not be able to play with her anymore?

My fears were answered when I tried to call her later that day and her father yelled in the phone to never call his house again and that Kristen was not allowed to hang out with lezzies. Again with this lezzy stuff. What was a lezzy? I was too afraid to ask anyone, and it made me feel as bad as Ms. Jackson had made me feel in fourth grade. What was wrong with me? Why wasn't I normal? Why didn't these feelings ever go away?

THE FALLOUT FROM OUR DIRTY DANCING got worse with time, not better. Apparently, Kristen's parents talked to someone else in the neighborhood and the story leaked out, as such stories always seem to do in small neighborhoods. The following week on the bus, most of the boys taunted me and called me a "lezzy" and told the other kids not to sit next to me. I remember feeling very dirty and isolated, and Kristen was sitting on the other side of the bus looking just as isolated as I felt.

I decided that day that whatever a lezzy was, I was *not* one. I would not let these boys make fun of me and call me names that meant nothing to me but hurt so badly. Amazingly, Kristen and I stayed friends, and we would talk and hang out whenever her father was not around.

We talked about what a lezzy was and what had happened between us. After doing some major research in a *Teen Beat* magazine article (investigative journalists we were not), we decided that we were going through a common phase that all adolescent girls go through.

This was a huge relief to both of us and we were able to resume our friendship, although it seemed to me much more restrained than it had ever been before. We began focusing on makeup and fashion and the cute boys in the neighborhood who wanted to play "seven minutes in heaven" with us, whatever that was. We didn't talk about the feelings ever again; we did not acknowledge them in any way after we learned that they would go away.

Even as I read the article and laughed with Kristen and we breathed a huge sigh of relief, I knew deep inside that those words didn't mean the same thing to me. A sense of dread planted its seed that day, a fear and concern that would grow with each passing day. It wasn't going away, not because a teacher yelled at me or a father screamed at me or boys called me names or *Teen Beat* said it should.

I was right. Those feelings didn't go away, even though I lied and said I liked boys. But even years later, no boy ever felt the same way pressed up against me as Kristen had or caused that electricity between my legs the way I had felt it that night. I never talked about it again, because I wasn't a lezzy and I didn't want to go to hell. I was normal, damn it, at least on the outside. No one needed to know what went on inside my head as long as my outward actions appeared normal.

Trouble was, the older I got, the harder appearing normal became.

6

Hurting Myself

I TURNED THIRTEEN A MONTH after Lee had attempted to rape me. This rite of passage that normally would bring about a huge, happy party was not celebrated in my family, because there was no longer anything normal about me. Instead, I was sitting in the living room on my father's brown La-Z-Boy chair watching TV. This was routine; for the past month I had been pretty quiet and very depressed. My brother and my cousin Thomas came in and began to give me shit, calling me stupid names, trying to get me out of the chair so they could watch TV.

Thomas was the son of my parents' friends Ben and Carol, whom we referred to as our uncle and aunt. Like my Uncle John's family, Uncle Ben's family wasn't my blood family, but we grew up with their sons Thomas, who was near Jimmy's age, and Eric, who was a year younger than me, as if they were our family. They lived next door to us when we lived in Wilson, where I was born, and we went on vacation with them every year. After we moved out of Wilson, they moved to Stroudsburg, so we didn't see them as often. When I was younger, I loved going to their house, because it was a long road trip from our house, and I had the biggest crush on Thomas. He was so cute and sweet.

Since he wasn't my *real* cousin, I never felt weird about it. He and my brother Jimmy were really close and kept in touch throughout their lives. Thomas would come and stay with us often. But today, Thomas was being a jerk, just like Jimmy was.

I refused to leave the chair, yelling back at them from a bottomless well of anger, shame, and regret. They picked up the chair and carried it to the front door, where my brother promptly put his end down to open the door. They proceeded to tip the chair over and dump me onto the porch. I landed on my knees and began to cry. They were both cracking up and then slammed the door in my face. That was it. I had had it. I began to run.

I didn't know where I was going, but I was leaving, running away. I ended up at my friend's house up the street and told her parents what had happened and that I wanted to run away. They let me use their phone; I called a friend from the roller rink, who said she would come and get me. Thirty minutes later she picked me up. I told her that I had been thrown out of my house and asked if I could stay with her. We drove back to her house in silence, and when we arrived, I went right to her room and sat listening to Prince's "When Doves Cry."

She told me that her mom said I would not be able to stay with them, so I had better call my mother. My mom had just started working at a fitness center in Easton, her first job ever. I called her there, told her what had happened, and cried as she told me to "get your ass home right now!"

AS MY FRIEND DROVE ME HOME, it began to get dark and I had this feeling inside that I had never had before: I was so depleted of hope and felt almost vengeful, like I was going to show them all. I got home and no lights were on, so I knew my brother and cousin had left. I entered the house and went right to my parents' liquor cabinet. I searched through bottles of whiskey, vodka, and other colored bottles until I came upon one with peaches on it that read "schnapps." I liked peaches, and schnapps sounded, I don't know, kind of warm and fuzzy, so I grabbed the bottle and went to the counter. I poured the thick contents into a glass and took a huge gulp without even sniffing it. It was bittersweet as it splashed onto the back of my throat in a wild peach-flavored rush tinged with the short flash of burn that I would always associate with alcohol.

I kept pouring and drinking, pouring and drinking, until that familiar feeling of euphoria came back to me, and soon I was high as a kite and began crying uncontrollably. Memories came rushing back to me in bits and pieces as I replayed the events of the past month. I was so scared and so lonely. I felt as though I had no one to turn to, no way to talk about the shit that was in my head. I had all these emotions but no words to attach to them.

I couldn't understand what was wrong with me. I only knew something bad had happened and it was all my fault. I went to the kitchen cabinet where my parents kept their prescriptions and grabbed two pill bottles that were sitting on the shelf. One was the Valium that my mother had been prescribed after I was born. I opened the bottle and watched with glassy eyes as thirty little yellow pills fell into my tiny hand. I stared at them for a while, remembering my mother saying quite often, "These are the pills I take for my nerves because of you."

Resentment filled my body and chills ran up my neck as I placed my hand to my mouth and tipped my head back, washing down the pills with another shot of peach schnapps. A bitter taste filled my mouth and I thought I would vomit. It passed and I went to the next bottle, which held my grandmother's blood-pressure pills. There were fifteen left in the bottle, and I washed them down with yet another shot of peach schnapps.

I really didn't know what I was doing. I didn't want to die or anything. I just wanted it all to stop. I couldn't stand the silent horror I had been living in for the past month. I went to the phone and proceeded to call everyone I knew, mumbling slurred "Good-bye's," "I'm sorry's," and "I love you's" to all my friends and, finally, my mother at work. When she heard my voice shaking and slurred, she knew something was wrong.

I told her I took all the pills and drank almost a bottle of peach schnapps. Suddenly, my mother's panic-stricken voice told me to calm down and that an ambulance would be there shortly. While she called our neighbors, I got off the chair I was sitting in and almost fell. My balance was off, my head began to swim, and the kitchen started to move. I tried walking, but I felt like I was in a fog and quicksand was dragging at my feet.

Just as I was about to fall, I gripped the sides of the sink and counter. I heard sirens in the distance. The front door opened almost in slow motion as two neighbors came in. They put my arms around their necks and carried me out the door. I was so incoherent by this time that I have no idea what I was saying to them. I do remember entering the warm spring air and seeing all our neighbors outside looking at this spectacle I was making, whispering to each other, "I don't know; she looks sick."

The ambulance pulled into our parking pad. Three emergency medical technicians (EMTs) came out and took me from my neighbors, putting me on a flat board and

Blackout Girl

into the back of the ambulance. My mother pulled up at that moment and ran toward me. I remember seeing the fear and tears in her eyes just as an EMT made me drink a thick black substance that made my mouth water and my stomach churn.

Almost immediately, I leaned over and vomited this nasty black substance with bits of yellow and peach schnapps into a bucket and then blacked out. The next thing I remember, I woke up in a hospital room in the intensive-care unit (ICU) with tubes everywhere and machines surrounding me. I could barely see the blurry images before me, but as I began to focus, I saw my father, my mother, both of my brothers, and my grandmother standing in front of me. Just as I tried to speak, I heard a loud beeping noise and two doctors ran into the room.

Through a fog I heard one of them yell, "You have to leave; we're losing her."

Then everything faded to black.

I WOKE UP SEVERAL HOURS LATER to find my family surrounding me again, all looking very tired and stressed out. I asked what happened, and my mother began to cry. My father said my blood pressure had dropped dangerously low and they had lost me for a couple of seconds.

My family had watched me die, even if it was only for a few seconds. Their greatest fears had come way too close to being real for anyone to deal with, and once again, it was all my fault. The pain in their bloodshot eyes was my doing. I couldn't look at them. I turned my head and spaced out. I had to emotionally check out or I would have gone insane.

I believe that when bad things happen and your mind can't begin to comprehend them, something inside you takes over to keep you safe. I left myself again in that hospital room, just as I had done a month earlier in the courtroom.

I was taken from the ICU to the sixth floor of Lehigh Valley Hospital, also called the mental or psych ward. I spent my entire summer there with other kids like me who had tried to kill themselves, some who were just plain crazy like the one girl they had locked up in a small room on twenty-four-hour suicide watch—she was in restraints and you could see her through a small window at the top of the door—and others who just sat in the corner and didn't speak at all. I knew I didn't belong there, and for the life of me, I could not figure out how the hell I had gotten there, because I didn't even really know why I took all the pills. I just knew deep down something was wrong, but I couldn't associate feelings or words with what was going on with me, so I let my actions speak for me.

I can honestly say that I had absolutely no feeling whatsoever; the phrase "I don't know" became my mantra. I seriously could not feel anything; I was numb. The doctors would ask a million and one questions, and I had no answers for any of them. "I don't know," I would mumble and look down at my hands folded neatly in my lap. I wasn't lying. I really *didn't* know anything. I didn't know why all of a sudden I couldn't articulate a sentence, or why the person I used to be seemed so far buried that I would never see her again. And I definitely didn't know why I felt so apathetic about everything.

I didn't know and I didn't care. I quickly learned all the right things to tell the doctors, and I was released after two months with a clean bill of mental health, although I had not dealt with anything. I had no basis for conversation about the events that had occurred the night of the attempted rape or any of the feelings that surrounded me in the dark.

I TRULY BELIEVE THAT WHEN YOU ARE YOUNG and something traumatic happens to you, your mind finds a way of protecting you. Just as I was able to detach in the court-room during Lee's hearing, I now found I had this ability to detach on cue. It became a survival instinct, a sanity tool.

If something even remotely struck me as scary or unsafe, I simply detached. I would often lie under men as they entered my body, never allowing them to enter my eyes or my soul. I detached out of fear, out of ignorance, and out of total lack of self. When I did start having sex around age fifteen, I spent many nights and many years afterward being an outlet for men and never truly learning the real meaning of intimacy. I thought I was supposed to not enjoy sex, that there was no real pleasure in it for me. I thought that if I didn't do it, something was wrong with me and the men would hurt me physically or, worse, emotionally by telling stories about me.

I know now that I never wanted to have sex with men, that my primary physical attraction was and will always be for women, but after the experiences of my youth, I was petrified to travel down that path again. Physical wounds heal and we can deal with them. They are easily treatable with medication and bandages, and we know that with treatment they will heal beneath the bandages. But emo-tional scars are much more complex; they enter a being in ways I can barely articulate and come out in all kinds of destructive ways that are not easily definable. They stay with us for life no matter how much we journal, see counselors, cry, scream. They are always there, somewhere beneath the smile as a reminder of the past.

AFTER MY OVERDOSE, I began hitting my parents' liquor cabinet on a daily basis, making crazy concoctions with the booze in all the big bottles. I would drink large glasses of nasty tasting liquor; they were like experiments. What will the yellow stuff taste like today? I had no idea what I was doing. I would take the contents of four or five different bottles and mix them in a large glass until the glass was almost full and then top it off with a splash of soda or orange juice. I didn't care how bad it tasted; I just wanted the feeling it produced.

That feeling, once so foreign, now so familiar, would make my head spin. It helped to numb the pain and quiet the noise in my head for a while, and that was all I cared about. I just wanted to forget everything. And feeling? Well, feeling was no longer an option for me, so whenever a feeling came up, I medicated it with whatever was around. If nothing was around, well, then I learned how to punish myself by inflicting pain.

Today they call this self-mutilating or self-injurious behavior, but back then, there were no names for this behavior. I couldn't totally avoid my feelings, so if I couldn't get drunk or high, then I would do anything else I could to halt the feelings. I would detach and float off into a beautiful daydream where my life was perfect and there were no issues. Or I would jump on my bike or roller skates and take off. But then the feelings would accumulate inside me, brewing slowly inside my gut until I was filled with a mix of emotions that I could no longer stuff inside. Then I would erupt, and if someone were around me, God help them, because they received the brunt of my volcanic emotional vomit. To keep from these inconvenient emotional outbursts that would raise the eyebrows of my parents and friends, I would reach for other means to release the pain. After all, I wanted to appear normal, whatever the hell that was.

When the memories of what had happened to me surfaced or any other feelings came up at all, always in really odd ways, ways that I could never actually articulate, I just felt awful. So I would cut myself with razors from my bathroom. I hated myself deeply and felt I was the cause of my own pain. For some reason, inflicting more pain upon myself somehow made it better.

It was a release that I could neither explain nor avoid. I would lock myself in the bathroom and remove a blade from my razor. At first I simply dragged the blade lightly up and down my forearm, just barely touching the surface. It sent tingles up and down my body. Then the thoughts came, the dark thoughts that lingered somewhere in the back of my mind but I could never really pull to the surface long enough to grasp, to understand.

I just knew the thoughts were there, and they produced a great deal of anxiety and fear in me. I couldn't handle that feeling, so as soon as they began to surface I put pressure on the blade. Scraping it, dragging it, slower and slower across my skin until it pierced my flesh and tiny streams of blood spilled out of my arm. Somehow this made it better. It was like I was releasing the demons from my head out through my arm.

As I watched the blood flow out of my self-inflicted wound, the bad feelings, the anger, and the anxiety flowed out of me. All the feelings and words that I couldn't make come out of my mouth flowed freely from my arm and disappeared as quickly as they came. After a couple of cuts like this, a sense of calm came over me that was incredibly peaceful. I would stop and then clean myself up with peroxide and a bandage. I would wrap my forearm with an

Ace bandage and walk out of the bathroom with the ability to breathe again. My parents and brothers would see the bandage and ask me what had happened, and I would make up some lame excuse like "I fell" or "I hurt my arm."

No one ever asked to see under the bandage. Sometimes I wondered whether they knew or had any idea. Maybe they were too scared to want to know the truth, so they just believed me and walked away on their own path of denial of how truly fucked up I was and how utterly helpless they were to control me.

SOMETIMES WHEN I GOT ANGRY I would skip the bathroom and go into my brothers' room and blast AC/DC or Led Zeppelin songs on the stereo. The boys had a strong wooden ladder that connected to their bunk beds, and as this powerful rage would come over me, I had to release it somehow. So I would punch the flat side of the wooden ladder. As soon as I started punching, I could not stop.

All this anger and rage would flow through my body like electricity, and I would punch harder and harder. With each blow I delivered to the ladder, I released the rage inside of my tiny body. I would do this until I collapsed onto the bed in sheer exhaustion. The anger would be gone, the rage released, and my hands would be so swollen that I couldn't distinguish one of my knuckles from another. It would just be one big, red, swollen mound of flesh.

Blade or bloody knuckles, it never seemed to matter; the same type of calm would come over me, and I would be able to make it through another day.

No one ever asked me about those knuckle bruises, either. My family knew I was fucked up, but they had no idea what to do with me. They didn't know what questions

Blackout Girl

to ask. My father tried to put me in therapy several times, but I just couldn't talk.

I didn't like to sleep. The dark scared me, so I kept the lights on, kept myself awake and watched movies or listened to music all night. I began to stay up all night, every night, and write morbid poetry about death. I remember going to school with little to no sleep and going through the day totally exhausted. Sometimes I would go to the nurse's office and sleep during the day. I processed some of my feelings through my writing. I remember one day my mother found one of my poems, read it, and became very scared. She asked me if I was okay and whether I wanted to die. I shrugged it off and told her no, that I was just doing some creative writing.

She never asked me about the poems again.

7

Dealing with Divorce

WHEN I WAS FIFTEEN, my mother was still working at the fitness club in Easton, close to where my father worked, and they would drive together. She had yet to get her driver's license, so my father would take her to work each night and pick her up on his way home. One night they stayed in the parking lot of our house for hours. My brothers, my grandmother, and I all knew something was wrong. Eventually they came through the door, my mother first, sobbing.

She fell into my grandmother's arms and cried, "He doesn't love me anymore. He wants a divorce." I watched my father come in slowly behind her, his head down in shame. He walked past us, went into his bedroom, and shut the door. My brothers went to my mother and began to console her, and Brian began to cry. I sat at the kitchen counter watching. I was numb but not surprised at all.

I had watched my parents' marriage coming apart for years, and while I seemed to be the only one who noticed, I pretended to be shocked. I got off the kitchen stool, walked into my parents' bedroom, and found my father sitting on the bed. I sat with him and put my arms around him. I loved my father deeply, and I wanted him to know that I knew and it was okay. I couldn't really say any of that, so I just hugged him as tightly as I could.

He decided to move out and live in Easton with my Uncle John, who had a large home with a spare room and an apartment on the top floor. I was very sad to see my father leave. I didn't want him to go.

My father called us every day. My brothers were very angry at him and rarely bothered with him. They were off doing their own things—by now, drinking and experimenting with harder drugs. They took my mother's side, if there was even a side to take. I clearly favored my father. He always treated me so well. He loved me and always provided a good home for us. I knew this and was the only one in the household who told him so.

I remember as a little girl curling up on his soft brown chair and falling asleep while watching TV. He would scoop me up off the chair and carry me all the way upstairs to bed. He would kiss my forehead and tell me he loved me while he tucked me in. I never went to bed without hearing my daddy tell me he loved me. It's another of the rare warm-fuzzy memories I kept close.

After he moved out, my dad made sure to pick me up and take me out to dinner at least once a week. And to this day, whenever I speak to my father or see him, we never part without saying "I love you" to each other.

MY MOTHER WAS A MESS. She cried day and night. She became very bitter and extremely angry. My mother was slowly deteriorating. I came home one day and found her highly intoxicated at the kitchen counter. I took the glass out of her hand, poured its contents into the kitchen sink, and carried her to bed, where I sat her up and took her shoes off. She clung to me, saying how my father was a bastard and loved someone else. I slowly pushed her down on the pillow and pulled up the covers. I kissed her on the forehead as my father had done to me so many times, told her it would be okay, and told her I loved her. She fell asleep.

The next day she woke up and began to pack. When I asked her what she was doing, she simply said, "I cannot handle this. I can't go through this and try to raise the three of you at the same time. I am leaving and your father will just have to come back and deal with this mess he has caused."

That night my father came back from my uncle's house and my mother went to live there instead. My grandmother also moved out and got her own apartment. My father worked very long hours, which allowed us kids to roam free and do whatever we pleased. We stayed out very late and rarely went to school. Our home life was no longer family-like but more a place where we all slept and occasionally ate. My father did the best he could while he tried to get his life back together. My father took on the entire debt that they had incurred during the relationship, and my mother got off free. She didn't even pay him support for keeping all three of us, which I found odd. My father had a great deal of guilt; she knew this and used it to her advantage.

I called my mother every day to see how she was, and with each passing day she grew more bitter and more angry, which seemed to give her a different kind of strength. She finally got her driver's license, purchased a car, and began searching for an apartment.

She also expected me to call her every day to report what my father was doing. I was never comfortable with this. She spoke horribly of my father as they went through the divorce proceedings. She never once came to pick me up and take me to dinner or anything like that. She never once came to see us.

8

First Roach

AT FIFTEEN, I was working weekend mornings doing food preparation at a restaurant within walking distance of home. It was an okay job if you didn't mind the masses of roaches that raced across the cutting board next to the vegetables I was to prepare for the buffet. Every once in a while, I would be in midslice and one would run across the counter. I would try to catch it with the knife blade. They were too quick for me, though, so every time I slammed the blade down, I just missed the little buggers by a hair. Roaches like the dark, so you know it is bad when they come out during the daylight. It usually means the place is near infestation if you see them in broad daylight. My boss was this large man with snow-white hair who sat at the bar for hours smoking and watching the 700 Club on TV. It wasn't too bad a job, and it gave me money that I needed for smokes and clothes.

There was a little convenience store right across the street from the restaurant. When I was younger, I had frequented this store to purchase smokes for my parents and candy and ice cream for me.

Now I was able to buy cigarettes from them because the clerks just thought I was getting them for my parents

like usual. Back then it was commonplace for a child
to go into a store and purchase smokes for her parents
because the rules about selling to minors weren't as strict.
I still always got nervous when I bought them, wondering whether the clerk would notice that my parents
had "switched brands," since they both smoked Benson &
Hedges Ultra Light 100's, but I took up Marlboro Lights.

ONE DAY AFTER WORK I bumped into Keith and Sam, two
of my brothers' older friends, outside the store. We made
small talk for a while, and I asked what they were doing
for the rest of the day. They both just shrugged and said
they would probably head up to the lounge. In school, I
had heard about the "lounge," a place in the woods where
the older kids went to party and get high. I was immediately intrigued. I had always wondered what it was like
there and desperately wanted to hang out with the older
kids in my school. With an immediate sense of self-assur-
ance, I pulled out the paycheck I had just received, held
it out in front of them and said, "I just got paid. If you
can cash this check for me, I'll buy some pot for us." They
looked at each other with surprised smiles before Sam
shrugged and said, "Hell yeah, I have a bank account in
town we can use to cash that and get some dope."

"Cool, let's go," I said. As I jumped into the back of
Keith's car, I was elated that they were letting me go with
them. I had never smoked pot before, but I knew both my
brothers were doing it. I always wondered what was so
funny and could never understand why they ate so much.
Even though each of us had our own set of friends, they
kind of all blended together at times, and later in high
school we all ended up hanging out with one another,
especially with Brian and me only one year apart in

school. I had seen my brothers come home with bloodshot eyes, laughing and eating everything in the kitchen. I was excited to see what all the mystery was about.

We went into town and pulled up at a bank. I signed the check over as I had done a bunch of times for my dad in the past. I didn't have my own bank account, and my dad always cashed my checks. I started to think up lies in my head to explain why I didn't need this check cashed. I would just say a friend cashed it and we went shopping. I handed the check over to Sam and he handed it to the teller. He handed the cash back to me. There was $45 in cash from my two weeks of work. He asked me how much pot I wanted. I never thought of that; I never thought about how much I should get as I had never bought it before. He said he could get a dime bag for $20, and I said that would be fine. I had no idea what a dime bag was and thought to myself, "Why does a dime cost $20?" I just handed him the money as he pulled up to a house. "I'll be right back, wait here," Sam said and then disappeared into the house.

WHEN SAM RE-EMERGED TEN MINUTES LATER, Keith looked over at him and simply asked, "Are we good?" Sam's face broke out into a large smile as he pulled out a long roll of what looked like oregano wrapped in a lunch bag. They were the same lunch bags that I used to carry my sandwiches in for school. Except this bag was rolled up into a dime-size cylinder. It dawned on me then, "Oh, so that is why they call it a dime bag." I busted out. They both just glanced at me in the backseat and laughed as Sam took off toward our school. Sam handed Keith the bag, "Pack one up, brother." Keith opened the ashtray and pulled out a thick metal object. It had a long cylinder that was bright red. A shiny silver tip with an opening was at one end. Opposite the red cylinder was a mini-bowl that stuck out on top. Keith filled the bowl with the pot, then put the silver tip in his mouth. He held the end of the bowl with one hand as he took a lighter and sparked a flame into the pot inside. I heard a crackling sound as a little white stream of smoke rose up from the bowl. I was fascinated watching him do this.

After about a minute, Keith blew a large puff of smoke out of his mouth and began to cough hard. Instantly a sweet, musky grass scent filled the air. It was intoxicating. I asked if he was okay. Sam turned to me and said with a smirk, "You gotta cough to get off, kid." I just stared back at him as Keith twisted around toward me to hand me the bowl and lighter. "Your turn," he said. I must have looked fearful, because he pulled the pipe back and asked, "Is this your first time? I don't want your brothers getting pissed at me."

"No, no," I said. "I've done this before, actually with my brothers. No, it's fine. They won't care." I lied and shook my head emphatically. He handed me the pipe and I put the silver tip in my mouth right away, imitating what he had just done, and then lit the bowl. I didn't want him to see that I was a novice, so I did this quickly and without thinking. Suddenly I was inhaling a large amount of smoke. It hit my mouth with a rush of sweet bitterness and filled my lungs. I was used to cigarette smoke, but this was different. It was smoother and stronger than any cigarette I ever smoked. I immediately began to cough, my eyes started to water like crazy, and my head felt a little tingly. There is a common myth that most people don't get "high" on their first time smoking pot. I think this is bullshit, because after I hit the pipe about five more times, I realized that this myth certainly would not apply to me.

THE "LOUNGE" WAS LOCATED BEHIND OUR SCHOOL in a development full of big, nice houses that I knew housed many of the popular kids in our school. Some of my friends lived there. A wooded area was at the end of the neighborhood. As we pulled up, I noticed a couple of cars parked near the road, and I figured they were other kids there doing the same thing we were about to do. My eyes felt squinty, like I was being exposed to a really bright light, and my whole body felt sort of numb. A feeling of peace came over me, and I found myself extremely happy all of a sudden, like nothing mattered. I opened the door, and when I went to step out, I felt as though I had accidentally misjudged a step and lost my balance. I bent over and began laughing hysterically in my head, although nothing came out of my mouth for a good minute. Then I burst into real laughter as I slowly brought my body back up in alignment. My friends were just looking at me laughing out loud. Keith said, "Umm, I think you're wasted, dude." I just laughed and followed them into the opening of the woods. Everything looked clearer, and the colors around me seemed brilliant. I felt so at peace and pleasantly happy as I floated through the woods toward a clearing where there was a dirty old couch, two worn chairs, and a box that served as a table.

There were a couple of other guys that I recognized from school there smoking and drinking. I was the only female, which didn't bother me so much. I liked being around guys, and many times I felt like one of the guys. I was often crass and swore a lot, so many boys discounted me as a hot chick they could hook up with and just saw me as Jimmy's or Brian's little sister. This worked very well for me, since my experience with guys was not too good anyway, but it did at times leave me feeling unpretty and awkward, especially when the pretty girls were around and I noticed the different way the guys acted around them.

We hung at the lounge for several hours smoking almost all the pot I had purchased. I wanted to share it with them so they would think I was cool and would want to hang out with me again. Eventually they drove me home.

I WAS HIGH AS A KITE AND STARVING. I went into the kitchen and started aimlessly sifting through the cabinets looking for anything edible. I eventually took a pizza out of the freezer and decided that would be the perfect meal. I loved those nasty cheap frozen pizzas that tasted more like cardboard than actual pizza—there was something about them. I was routing through the spice rack to hook up my pizza when my eyes landed on a jar of dry-roasted peanuts, one of my other all-time favorite snacks. I pulled them out and began shoveling handfuls into my mouth as I powdered my pizza with garlic and oregano. Then a brilliant lightbulb went off in my head. What if I put peanuts on the pizza? I love pizza and I love peanuts, so it made perfect sense to combine these items in my foggy pot-induced haze. I littered the top of the pizza with dry-roasted peanuts and placed the pizza in the oven.

I wolfed the pizza down in what felt like two and a half minutes. I can't ever remember being so freaking hungry. I could have eaten five of them. I didn't even wait until I'd swallowed one bite before my lips were over another bite. Turns out that dry-roasted peanuts aren't too bad atop a nasty frozen pizza. It became one of my favorite meals to eat after burning a bowl, which also became a weekly and sometimes daily habit after my introduction that day.

AFTER EATING MY PIZZA, I locked myself into my bedroom, because I didn't want my dad to see the red slits my eyes had become. I had stolen my brother's Tom Petty CD from his room, shut my lights off, and lain on my bed as I got lost in the words and rhythms to "Free Falling." The song was brilliant and made total sense to me. This was my introduction into a whole new realm of music. I went from listening to Debbie Gibson to Pink Floyd almost overnight. It was a great evolution, and my inner flower child was born. I loved pot, the freedom it gave me. The feeling of being so happy was just want I wanted. I couldn't find happiness on my own, so a chemically generated high that made me smile was just fine with me. It made me forget the pain, the memories, the hidden bad things that lingered, and it just let me laugh.

Except, of course, for the times that it didn't. I realized very early on that I was not good at mixing things. The first time I tried to get high while drunk, it didn't end well. About fifteen minutes after smoking up, I felt the entire room begin to swirl and not in a good way. I had a rude awakening and ended up face-down in the cold porcelain bowl for hours. I tried and tried to smoke pot and drink but rarely achieved success. I always got sick—mainly because I drank so much that adding an additional depressant to the mix just didn't sit well with me. The only time I could get high and not get sick was if I only had a beer or two, and trust me, that was a very rare occasion. However, this didn't stop me from trying. Like a good addict, I tried all kinds of combinations and always somehow managed to convince myself that I would not get sick if I just took a couple of hits. There's that definition of insanity again. So instead, I just got used to puking a lot.

9

Losing Alex

LEX, STACY, AND I WENT OUT and drank together. We were just turning fifteen, and people in our school had started to have parties, so we went out on weekends and got hammered. We would lie, telling one set of parents we were staying over at the other's house, and then go out all night to parties. We drank nasty beer like Busch pounders and Milwaukee's Best, which we kindly referred to as Beast. I was already smoking cigarettes daily. My parents knew and occasionally let me smoke in the house and around them.

Alex and I went out to stores and shoplifted all the time. Her parents dropped us off at the local mall, and we would clean house. I think it was the whole adrenaline rush, the fear of being caught and the excitement of doing something bad. We came home with hundreds of dollars worth of stuff that we didn't need: makeup, clothing, and anything we could hide in our purses or under our clothes.

Stacy, Alex, and I had met in fourth grade when my family first moved to Bath. My family then moved to the trailer park a few miles from town, and I went to a different middle school. When we moved back to Bath, I entered seventh grade and was reunited with Stacy and Alex. I was so excited to be with them again.

I loved being around Stacy, mainly because I knew deep down she had the same type of feelings that I had for girls. She was clearly a lesbian even back then, but of course none of us knew what that meant. We just knew that people thought it was gross for girls to like girls, so we never spoke of such things. But in our eyes a whole different story was told. I knew Stacy and I shared that, and without ever speaking of it, I found solace in her presence.

Alex, who quickly became my best friend in the world, was another story. I think she had similar feelings and might have ended up at least bisexual, but at fifteen, she was boy-crazy to the max. She always had a million crushes on boys. She lived about five miles from me, so on Fridays I would go over and spend weekends with her.

ALEX'S PARENTS WERE WEIRD. They were always nice and welcomed me into their home, but there was always a negative energy there that I couldn't explain. They would make us corn cakes for breakfast with butter and grape jelly. I loved those things, and to this day, when I pass them in the bread aisle, I think of Alex and early mornings at her house.

Alex and I had a lot in common. She had feelings like I did and expressed them similarly. While we never discussed the feelings, we were able to unconditionally accept one another without really saying why. She had pain, too. Someone had hurt her deeply, too.

We began to open up to each other. She was one of the first people I was able to really start to tell things to, especially the dark things from my past. She confided in me that terrible things had happened to her sexually as a child. We found a gentle comfort in one another. We didn't speak of these things often, but simply knowing that we understood each other was of such comfort to both of us. I knew her pain ran deep just like mine, and she was haunted at night just like I was. I started staying over at Alex's more often.

ALEX AND MY BROTHER BRIAN began dating, which was odd at first, but after a while I became okay with it.

My father started dating Pat, a woman whom none of us had ever met. He used to work with her. My mother immediately assumed it had been going on for years and that was why they broke up. It wasn't the reason, but she needed someone outside herself to blame, so it didn't have to be about her and, therefore, she didn't have to deal with it at all.

My brothers and I began to have big parties at our house, because my father began spending nights at Pat's house. Our house became party central. This is when all my brothers' friends and my friends really started comingling and we were all partying together. A lot more drugs were coming into our house now, and we always had plenty of beer and pot. On average, we would have fifty or more people crammed into our house while my dad was out.

ALEX CALLED ME ONE NIGHT from her bedroom; she was really upset. She and my brother had broken up a couple of weeks prior, and a couple of us had skipped school and gotten caught. We had all skipped school that one day and gone over to Richard's house. Richard, who was a friend's cousin, was way older than we were and had two little girls. Alex had been hooking up with him at one point. We often went to his house to party after school and on the weekends, and he always bought us beer and got drugs for us.

Alex's parents were very angry, and she was grounded for a month. We each got three days out-of-school suspension, and I was grounded for a week. She began to talk to me about how she wanted to run away and asked me if I would go with her. Just thinking about jumping in her dad's van and taking off for the West Coast was a nice thought. We talked about where we would go, how much fun we would have, and how we would be free for the first time in our lives. She mentioned for the first time having a gun in the house and said we should take it with us, just in case. I was shocked and asked why her dad had a gun. She said he had a .22-caliber pistol for protection, and she knew where it was. There was also a wad of cash in the freezer, and we could take that with us, too.

At first I was playing along, until I realized how serious she was. I started to get a little nervous and began asking a bunch of questions. She was really upset and mentioned a couple of times that it would just be better if she killed herself. I talked to her for hours that night. I knew what she was feeling; I had been there myself so many times before. I told her it wouldn't solve anything and that we had so much more to do yet. We were both about to get our driver's licenses soon; she was going to be sixteen in a couple of months. Then we could go out all the time and escape from everything.

After a couple of hours, she seemed to calm down and began speaking more rationally. She said she was okay and thanked me for helping her out. We then made plans for me to go over and spend the weekend; even though she was grounded, her parents loved me and had said it was okay if I came over. I told her I would see her the next day at school, and we got off the phone.

We always met by our lockers before homeroom in the morning. That morning she came over to my locker like normal and seemed to be in a great mood. We talked for a while and I admired a gold herringbone necklace she was wearing. I traced my finger along the necklace and told her that I really liked it. She brought her hands up behind her head, underneath her black hair, unhooked the chain, and placed it in my hands. She looked up at me and said, "Here, don't say I never gave you anything. Something to remind you of me."

Our eyes met and we smiled at each other as I thanked her. Just then, the bell rang and we quickly parted. I yelled to her that I would call her after school about coming over that night for the weekend. She smiled and ran off to class.

WHEN I GOT HOME FROM SCHOOL, while I was waiting for my father to get home from work, I packed to go over to Alex's for the weekend. As I finished, I was about to pick up the phone to call Alex when a friend from up the street came rushing into my house. He frantically asked me where Alex lived. I answered, "Sleepy Hollow Road in Bath. Why?"

He was red in the face and out of breath from running, and as he opened his mouth, I couldn't believe what came out. He said he had been listening to his father's radio scanner and something came across about a girl shooting herself on Sleepy Hollow Road in Bath. I froze and stared at him.

At the same time, my father walked in the door. I ran to him and said, "Dad, we have to drive to Alex's. I think something bad happened." I told him what my friend had just said as I rushed him out of the house and into his car.

WE DROVE THE FIVE MILES down to Alex's house in silence. It seemed to take forever to get there. As we turned onto her street, I saw police vehicles and crime-scene tape all around her house.

We drove by very slowly, and I saw her parents in the driveway of the neighbor's house looking terrified. My father stopped the car and asked what happened and explained that I was her best friend. The officer said there had been a terrible accident and that Alex had shot herself in the face with a .22-caliber automatic pistol.

I sat in the car in disbelief. All I could think was, "Oh my God; she did it." A tremendous amount of guilt over-came me as I recalled the phone conversation we had had the night before. I quickly replayed in my head each and every word she had said. My mind began racing. I thought I had talked her out of it. I thought she was okay. Oh my God, why didn't I tell someone? This is my fault.

All of a sudden her face came into focus in my mind. I recalled touching her herringbone necklace and her taking it off and saying, "Don't say I never gave you anything. Something to remind you of me."

I reached up to my neck and touched the necklace softly as tears spilled down my face uncontrollably. My father turned to me and tried to console me, but I didn't hear a word he said.

I just stared off past the police lights, past her parents' grief-stricken faces, past the trees surrounding the street. I heard nothing and only saw Alex's beautiful smile as she ran off to class that morning.

MY FATHER AND I DROVE HOME in total silence. I entered the house, and my brother Brian was in his room on his top bunk, just lying there. I walked in and climbed the first couple of rungs of the ladder and touched his head softly. The tears streaming down my face confirmed his thought that Alex was dead. He began to sob uncontrollably into his pillow. Then he looked up at me and said, "It's my fault. I shouldn't have broken up with her." I looked at him and shook my head no.

After all, it wasn't his fault; it was mine. I could have saved her; I could have told someone. But I didn't say any of that to him. I kept that deep inside, hidden with all my darkness. I felt the acknowledgment of it would make the empty pit that had already formed inside my soul bigger and deeper. Its depth was too painful for me to face. I walked out of the room and called my friends to tell them what had happened.

10

Mourning Alex

I WAS IN A ROBOTIC STATE, speaking in a monotone without much feeling as I went down the list of our friends and called them all to give them the horrible news about Alex. Several of us made plans to meet up with a friend who was babysitting that night. We arranged for plenty of alcohol and pot. I arrived there around 7 P.M.

We all sat in disbelief and quickly got inebriated. I don't remember much other than that I drank a lot and smoked pot. At some point during the evening, four of us—Megan, Jessica, Ann, and I—left the house in a drunken haze and stumbled toward the local pizza hangout. It was where everyone went after football games. We got there just as everyone arrived after a game. The place was packed, and as soon as we opened the door to walk in, it seemed like everyone stopped doing what they were doing to stare at us. The news had traveled, and everyone knew Alex was dead.

They also knew we were her closest friends. People began to rush up to us. People we had never even talked to before were looking at us with sympathy and asking if we were okay. What's worse, some of them just stared at us with looks of horrified pity on their faces. I was drunk and annoyed with this sudden rush of popularity. I didn't want to talk to anyone; I was loaded and just wanted iced tea and pizza.

Megan and I placed our orders and went to a table to wait for our pizza with Ann and Jessica. We sat there as person after person came up to us expressing their grief. It was annoying. People who never even knew Alex were making comments and looking at us. My friends and I began to get very angry. We decided to leave the pizza shop.

JESSICA AND ANN WERE WALKING UP THE HILL toward another friend's car to get us a ride, while Megan and I trailed behind. I was very drunk and stumbling up the hill when I realized I was walking alone. I turned to look back for Megan, only to find her next to a cop car.

The officer was placing handcuffs on her as she screamed at him. I quickly turned to look up at Jessica and Ann, who were watching in dismay. I heard them yell, "Storm, come on. Let's go!" Instead, I turned back toward Megan and the cops and went barreling down the hill after Megan. I wasn't going to leave her behind.

I approached one cop and began yelling in his face, "Let her go! What the fuck do you think you're doing with her?" The officer tried to restrain me, which made me angrier. The rage that lived deep inside the empty pit in me came flying up and out like a lion. I began swinging and kicking as fast as I could. Like a drowning child in a pool, I was fighting for my life. I landed quite a few kicks and punches on the two officers.

I was screaming at them. "Get off me, you fucking pig" was among the lovely comments that flew out of my mouth. They finally got my arms behind my back, threw me down onto the police car, and handcuffed me. Already a cold October evening, it had just started to rain. I felt the cold, wet metal of the cop car crash against my cheek as they threw me down.

It sobered me up slightly.

My head was spinning as they pushed me into the backseat next to a bewildered Megan. By now, a huge crowd stood outside the pizza place. They had watched everything. I saw Jessica's and Ann's dismayed faces as we drove past them toward the police station.

Megan was wiggling around next to me in the seat. When I looked over at her, I realized she had gotten out of her handcuffs and was attempting to open the car door. Of course, like all cop cars, in this one the handles had been removed from the inside so no one could escape. We arrived at the station, and the officers pulled us out of the vehicle. They were angry as they brought us into the station and threw us into separate holding cells. The cop I had hit first slammed the bars shut on my cell and glared at me as he walked away. Megan was in the cell next to mine, screaming at the cops.

I sat on the nasty white cot in utter disbelief, wondering what the hell had happened. I was very drunk and high and it was all a haze. My head was whirling as I slowly began to sober up enough to realize that I was in big trouble.

I WAS SCARED AND TREMBLING as I thought of Alex. My heart ached so bad and I began to feel all the pain I had attempted to cover up by drinking so much earlier. The chief of police came into the room. I knew him and he knew our parents; he was a very nice man. A couple months earlier, several of us had been busted during a football game for drinking wine coolers behind the school. The chief had called my father, who had been out but promptly sent his friends to pick me up at the police station. We didn't get into any legal trouble that night, just received a warning and were sent back to our parents.

Tonight, the chief also informed us that our parents had been called and were on their way. I sat there sobbing and calling out for Alex. What seemed like ten hours later, our parents arrived. They must have filled in the chief on what had happened that day, because when he came in again, his face was filled with empathy and compassion.

He unlocked the door to let me out of the cell and told me that my father was waiting for me. I was scared out of my mind and filled with so much pain and grief. I didn't want to face my father for fear of what would happen. I didn't want to feel what I was feeling inside; it was like someone was ripping my heart out of my chest. For a moment, I thought, "Alex is the lucky one. She doesn't have to feel this or deal with this."

Before leaving the holding area to meet up with my father, I asked the officer escorting me if I could use the bathroom. He led me to a small bathroom in the back of the building and said he would wait right outside for me. I entered the bathroom and saw myself in the mirror. My hair was all wet and messy, my face was bright red and blotchy from crying, my mascara had run all down my face, and I had black makeup everywhere. I looked almost as bad as I felt. I was frantic and didn't know what to do. I did not want to face my father.

I OPENED THE CABINET BELOW THE SINK and looked around at the various bottles of cleansers and materials. I didn't know what the hell I was looking for, but my hand stopped on a bottle of Drano. I slowly picked it up and opened it. My mind was racing, and I wanted all the thoughts and feelings to stop. I wanted it to end. I couldn't tolerate the pain any longer. I raised the bottle to my mouth and began to chug it. As the liquid splashed against my tongue, it immediately made my mouth water and made me want to vomit. It was very bitter and tasted like soap. I choked loudly as I tried to drink as much of it as I could.

I could hear the officer outside the door asking me if I was okay. After hearing no response, he came barreling through the door, only to find me kneeling on the floor gasping and choking with the Drano bottle in my hand. It quickly became obvious to him what I had done, so he picked me up and made me lean over the toilet as I began puking my brains out. My head was throbbing as chunks of pizza and bile spilled out of my mouth into the water. The water splashed up and hit me on my face. It was cold, and I remember it felt good.

I vomited for a good half hour.

The officer helped me to my feet. I could see the fear and disbelief in his eyes when he looked at me. Who knew what was going through his mind? He helped me get a drink of water and wash my face off, and then he walked me out to my father, who was standing there with no idea what had just happened. I slid down into a chair in the front of the police station as the officer informed my father what I had done. I saw my father's eyes grow huge as he looked over at me in shock.

My dad decided not to take me to the hospital since I had thrown up everything I had just ingested. I was grateful for that, since they would have probably committed me to the psych ward for trying to kill myself.

My father and I drove home in silence. At one point he looked over at me and asked if I wanted to die. I looked at him and lied. I said no, I did not want to die. Truthfully, I wanted to be anywhere other than where I was at that moment. I wanted to be with Alex, and yet I was so angry at her for leaving me here in pain. My dad never mentioned the night at the police station again.

ALL CHARGES AGAINST ME WERE DROPPED, thankfully, because I was facing some serious charges for a fifteen-year-old, including simple assault on a police officer, resisting arrest, disorderly conduct, and underage drinking. The officers felt sorry for us after they learned what had happened, and we went back to school on Monday as though it were any other day.

Instead of letting us go to classes, though, the school administrators called those of us who were Alex's friends into a room with a counselor who tried to "talk" to us about our feelings. None of us were really into dumping our feelings, but it was a nice distraction from class, so we all sat with this counselor all day. One of the guys in our group who had dated Alex a while back was really emotional, and finally he did start to break down. He got very angry, and for whatever reason, focused his anger on me and began yelling at me. He screamed that it was unfair that she was dead. Then he looked right at me and said, "I wish it would have been you instead of her." It was like a cold smack right to my jaw to hear him say the words I myself had been feeling deep down. He quickly regained his composure and started to cry, apologizing and hugging me. I returned the hug and said it was okay, but his words never really did leave my mind.

Word got out about everything I had done Friday night, and all day long people kept coming up to me, giving me high-fives and calling me Rocky. I enjoyed the attention, mainly because it made people fear me a little bit, which meant they would think twice before doing anything to me. I liked that feeling; it felt safe. I didn't want to be bothered by anyone. The pit in my stomach was over-whelmingly large, and I just wanted to be alone. I missed Alex so much it hurt inside, and a part of me wanted to be with her, wherever she was.

ALEX'S PARENTS DECIDED TO CREMATE HER right away and hold a very small ceremony. It was weird. They only invited five of Alex's friends: me, another girl who hung out with us occasionally but wasn't in our inner circle, and three girls Alex hadn't really hung out with recently, mainly because they were good students who didn't party. These were the only friends that Alex had ever taken home, so in her parents' minds, these were the only friends who should be at the ceremony. It really hurt my brother and the rest of Alex's friends to be excluded from the proper mourning. The ceremony was freaky, in a church with her urn and an enlarged picture of her. The church was empty other than us five and her parents.

11

Blackouts, Bulimia, and Burials

THE REST OF MY TIME IN HIGH SCHOOL was sort of a blur. I didn't care about anything anymore; everything inside of me had gone totally numb. I drank and smoked pot every chance I could get. I never drank just one drink. I do believe that I had an unhealthy chemical reaction to alcohol. When I ingested one drink, something inside my body and mind kicked in, and I couldn't stop. And when I say I couldn't stop, I totally mean that. It would take an act of extreme willpower for me not to get drunk once I had one drink. So I drank until I was hammered.

I was blacking out often, waking up and simply not remembering pieces of the night before. I would go out with all my friends and, as usual, drink way too much and smoke pot until the world around me was engulfed in darkness and the pain in my soul ceased, if only for a few hours.

One night we were all at a huge party and I was, of course, hammered out of my mind. I woke up the next day in an unfamiliar bedroom, on the floor next to a bed with a football player's arm slung over my torso as he slept next to me. I had apparently had sex with him the night before. My best friend was in the bed above me with another one of the players, with whom she had done the same thing. I didn't remember doing it, but it was pretty evident by the lack of clothing I had on, and later someone told me that I had.

It was like the night was a big puzzle. I would often call my friends to try to gather up the pieces I was missing to gain the full picture. I usually ended up feeling ashamed or embarrassed, because I would do stupid shit while I was hammered.

Another night I was hanging out with my friend Ann, drinking and smoking pot, this time with a couple of guy friends from the wrestling team at school. We were in the one guy's car partying. Ann and he got out of the car to take a walk, leaving me in the backseat with the other guy. We knew them pretty well and had hung out with them before without any issues, so I did not really expect what came next.

Out of the blue, he started kissing me and grabbing me everywhere. I kept trying to talk and to look around to find Ann. I had only drunk a couple of beers at this point but wasn't drunk. I had no interest in this guy in any way other than as a friend. But he persisted. He eventually got on top of me, and as I continually said, "No, please stop; I don't want to," he ignored me and fucked me anyway. He was much bigger and stronger than I was, so I stopped fighting and detached from my body, from his weight on top of me, from the car, and once again floated above to my safe place. I wondered why I should even bother using my voice when it didn't make enough noise, use my force when it wasn't strong enough, and express my choice when it was clear I had none.

I remember that afterward, Ann came back and the two guys pulled away in the car I had just been violated in. I sat on the curb and sobbed uncontrollably. Once again, I had experienced this thing called sex, and it was nasty and dirty. There was nothing romantic or beautiful about it. I felt angry and jilted. I was so incredibly confused. I had seen movies and read stories about romance and love, but how they depicted sex was not any experience I had ever had. My experiences were either sexual assault or sex during blackouts, which I could not recall the next day. I had no idea what true love and true intimacy were.

I began drinking more and plunging deeper into the black pit that had formed in my gut. It was this empty space that resided inside of me and ached each and every day. The only thing that ever made the ache go away was getting totally annihilated—which I made sure I did on an almost daily basis.

THE ONLY CONTACT I HAD with my mother at this time was on the phone and occasionally face-to-face when I would ask my dad to take me to her apartment to see her. She never came to see me, not once. Whenever we spoke, she always found ways to tear down my father, which made me incredibly angry. She was always finding fault with every thing he did and blowing the smallest of his kind gestures out of proportion. I would stick up for him rigorously. After all, unlike Mom, who walked out and never looked back, Dad, who wasn't around a whole lot, at least bought groceries, picked me up when I needed a ride, and was willing to stick it out and try to be a parent. Of course, many of these thoughts never left the screaming room in my head; they never dared pass my lips into the phone receiver for her to hear. I couldn't hurt her like that; it was easier to just take what she dished out to me.

Our talks and my visits were never positive; she was always so incredibly judgmental and critical of my appearance. I was never skinny enough, my hair was never long enough, my makeup was a mess. Her constant berating of me just fueled the growing self-esteem issue that I had developed. Part of it was just normal teenage angst, but the rest came from my own beliefs that I was a bad person, which stemmed from the assault.

Being a teenage girl in America was hard enough without all the other compounding issues I had. Girls at school were highly competitive. If you didn't wear the right brand names and sizes of clothes, you were made fun of. One time after gym class, we were all coming back into the locker room to change out of our gym clothes, and a bunch of the more snobby rich girls went over to one of their own best friends, with whom they were apparently fighting at the time. They grabbed her Guess jeans to see what size they were. They were a size ten, and the girls held them up laughing and scream-ing, "Oh my god, you are like a cow." They told everyone in school. This girl was incredibly beautiful, with long, cascading red curly hair. She was by no means a heavy girl, just big-boned and in shape with no fat on her body anywhere. These girls were brutal. Of course, a week later they totally forgave her and were best friends again. So that, coupled with everything I read in fashion magazines and had seen on *Beverly Hills 90210*, told me that I better be a size four or smaller if I didn't want to be considered a cow.

I had a hard time maintaining my weight, though, because I drank a lot and loved to eat. So I began taking laxatives. A friend of mine in school told me about it, so I figured I would try it. It got to the point that no matter what I ate, I followed it with a little pink laxative pill. It didn't matter how skinny I was, I always felt fat. I was a big-chested girl, so even when I was tiny, I still appeared to be shapely because my breasts never went below a size D. I hated my body. I had no real connection to it. I detached from it most of the time anyhow, but when I did look in the mirror, I loathed what I saw.

I managed to stayed a size two and never thought taking the laxatives was a bad thing, since most of my friends also did it or threw up their meals altogether. I could never force myself to puke, though. I tried it a couple times thinking I could get rid of the calories quicker, but I just hated the act of vomiting. The burning, nasty bile taste in my throat and nose just grossed me out. I did enough puking when I was smashed, so I wasn't about to intentionally put myself through that.

I ALSO BEGAN SKIPPING SCHOOL CONSTANTLY. I just couldn't stand being there. Having to sit in classrooms for hours trying to focus on sociology or math seemed impossible. I couldn't be in my own skin and sober long enough to sustain a full day. Stacy and I would meet every day at our lockers and skip the last two periods of the day to go under this bridge by our school and get high. I was starting to get high before school, too, and leaving between classes to drink to make the day more bearable. I had no ambition, no fear, and no cares about anything.

Many of the kids in my school partied, so it wasn't like I was an outcast or anything. It wasn't just your stereotypical druggies with rock concert T-shirts and dirty hair who partied and did drugs in our school; it was the captain of the football team and other players, cheerleaders, and wrestlers. We went to a rural school, so there wasn't much to do except drive around on long, winding back roads, drink, do drugs, and get into trouble. And since our house had become the place to go for parties, the lifestyle just seemed to suit me fine. All I wanted to do was escape, run away, not feel a damn thing.

I couldn't bear my feelings and refused to deal with anything, so this cycle of drinking and drugging worked brilliantly for me. My class-cutting increased, and I was actively bulimic. Cutting and bulimia were two things I could have 100-percent control over at a time when my world was spinning completely out of control. It was an odd dichotomy for me, because in many areas I loved being totally out of control, because then I didn't have to feel the pain inside, yet I always tried to find a way to be in control without being in pain.

ACID BECAME THE HOT NEW THING in school during junior year, and a core group of us started hanging out and doing it pretty much every weekend. I loved the way it sent me into a twelve-hour state of total euphoria and skewed reality. You could drop a hit of acid at 7 P.M. and by 8 P.M. be so out of it and happy that you didn't care about anything. It seriously altered my state of being and I loved it; it was exactly what I desired.

One night in particular we were all over at Ann's house tripping on acid, and my friend Jason and I were lying outside in the front yard just staring up at the stars for hours. The stars danced for us, and we lay there laughing and talking about all kinds of philosophical things, like wondering whether we were alone in the universe and what life would be like on the moon and other planets.

Jason was a really cute guy who was older than me and had dated Megan on and off throughout high school. He was a really good wrestler but had a really bad drug habit and a serious anger management issue. He was known for flying off the handle and getting violent with people. I personally witnessed him take a wooden mallet from my kitchen one night and smash a friend's hand wide open, splashing blood all over our kitchen, which I later cleaned up. On another night with Megan and me in his car, he threatened to crash the car and kill us all because Megan was threatening to break up with him. He swerved violently all over the winding roads we were driving on. I thought I was going to die that night.

But on this night, under the stars, tripping on acid, he was beautiful and gentle. He was smart and sweet, and we just talked for what seemed like forever. Many moons and years away from that night, I would get a phone call and learn that he died in his sleep; during an alcohol-induced blackout, he choked on his own vomit.

ALL OF US WERE REALLY CLOSE, and in addition to hanging out every weekend, we also vacationed together at the beach each summer and went to the annual state wrestling championship where Jason and a bunch of our other friends competed.

Our school was well-known for having a winning wrestling team across the state of Pennsylvania. We won the state championship (States) several years in a row, and many of our wrestlers won their divisions each year. Our coach even won Coach of the Year several years in a row.

Each year the state championship was held in Harrisburg, Pennsylvania. It was the highlight of the year in our school and was a notoriously huge party vacation for students. My friends and I made it an annual event to pack up the cars and head up Route 81 for the "Balls to the Walls" party weekend.

During my senior year, we all packed up as usual in March for our trip. We made sure we had plenty of alcohol before we went. I purchased a case of Snapple Mango Madness Juice Drink and brought two half gallons of vodka, so we were all set. Stacy and I went in on an eighth of pot, and Megan, Jessica, and Ann got some coke. Several of our friends also scored some LSD, so we had enough to get us through the weekend.

Jessica, Ann, Megan, Stacy, and I blew off school on Thursday and arrived at the Howard Johnson hotel in Harrisburg around noon. We started drinking immediately, and once our other friends started showing up, the party really began. We took over the hotel because we occupied about ten rooms with just our friends alone. The first night we dropped acid and hung out in various rooms all night. We partied until about 5 A.M. While the wrestlers went off to compete, we all stayed back in our rooms sleeping. There was no stopping at States, so the minute we woke up, we started partying again. I woke up nauseated and still a little drunk from the night before. Stacy was firing up a bowl of weed next to me, and I rolled over and took it from her hand and hit it with all my might. After a few minutes, my hangover was released, and I was able to get out of bed. I popped open a Snapple and took two huge gulps out of the bottle, which I quickly replaced with vodka and shook up. I figured this was a good concealer for my alcohol, just in case the police showed up.

As the day gave way to night, the hotel filled with more and more people. Everywhere you went there were students partying; they spilled out of the rooms and into the halls, resulting in more than one visit from the hotel manager threatening to call the cops on all of us.

Jessica was dating Sam at this time, and they had a very volatile relationship. Sam was a huge partier and was known to get a little out of hand every once in a while. They fought constantly, and as the evening progressed, so did their most recent argument. Sam was pissed off at Jessica because he wanted to get more coke and she didn't. Stacy and I were in our room smoking pot when we heard Sam and Jessica fighting from outside the door. After a few minutes of screaming, Jessica came barreling into the room and slammed the door shut behind her. "Asshole!" she screamed as she locked the door. Sam began banging on the door and yelling for her to open it.

She sat down on the bed and fired up a bowl, ignoring the banging. Stacy and I just looked at each other and collectively rolled our eyes; we didn't feel like getting involved. After a few minutes, the banging stopped. We figured Sam just got over the argument and went away. Apparently he went down the hall and came upon a fire extinguisher encased in glass, which he promptly put his fist through in a fit of rage. We were clueless until we heard the alarm going off. We began rushing around the room trying to hide our stuff, because we knew the cops would show up any minute after the alarm sounded. The banging on the door came back, but this time Sam was screaming out in fear rather than anger. Stacy and I begged Jessica not to open the door, but she let him in anyway. As soon as she saw his hand bleeding, she rushed him into the bathroom to tend to his wounds. I glanced out into the hallway to see drunken students scattering like cockroaches into rooms as the alarm reverberated off the walls.

As we were hiding all the drugs and paraphernalia, the sliding glass door to our balcony opened up and three uniformed officers entered our room. "Shit," I thought to myself, "we are totally busted." Being the cocky smartass that I was, I immediately approached the officers and requested to see a search warrant. They politely told me to sit down as they surveyed the room. Some beer cans and one of my bottles of vodka were sticking out of a bag. After seeing the booze, the officers began asking us for our identification. I lied and said I didn't have mine. If I showed it to them, it would be obvious that it was altered to make it appear that I was twenty-one. They asked us our age, date of birth, Social Security number, and address. We each gave the information, and after all was said and done, we were each issued a citation for underage drinking. We didn't get arrested or hauled downtown like I thought we would, but they did confiscate the visible beer cans and the one bottle of vodka. After about an hour, they left, and more than fifteen students ended up being cited for underage drinking. It put a damper on the rest of the weekend, but at least the drugs were safe, and I still had half a case of Snapple left and a hidden bottle of vodka.

We stayed the rest of the weekend and kept a low profile while we continued to get hammered. A couple of months later, we all had to return to Harrisburg to the Dauphin County Courthouse for a court date. I tried to defend our group by stating that it was unfair that the police entered without a search warrant. The judge wasn't having it, and we all got fined and lost our licenses for thirty days.

More than a decade later, during the final phase of my job interview for my current job with Victim/Witness Assistance Program, this little incident would come back to haunt me. The district attorney interviewing me in the very same building where I attempted to defend my underage drinking waived the court docket in front of me after performing a background check on me. I was stunned; I had honestly forgotten that I had ever been to the courthouse before and had forgotten the incident altogether until he brought it up. He gave me the docket, and as I looked over the paperwork, the judge's name caught my attention because it was the county's current president judge who adjudicated my case. We had a little chuckle over it and chalked it up to juvenile antics that, thankfully, were far behind me now. But I was once again struck with how incredibly ironic my life was as I moved into my new office in that very courthouse.

DURING MY FRESHMAN YEAR and throughout the rest of my time in high school, a rash of driving under the influence (DUI) and freak accidents killed about eight of my classmates. I remember coming to school one day to learn that the girl who sat behind me in homeroom had died in a drunk-driving accident over the weekend. We weren't tight, but it still had a deep effect on me. I remember staring at her empty seat while the principal's voice came over the loudspeaker breaking the sad news. I went to the viewing; it was the first dead body I had ever seen.

It wasn't the first death I'd experienced though. That had happened in fourth grade, when my best friend David died in a sledding accident. Because I was only ten years old, my parents would not let me attend David's funeral. They thought I was too young to handle it. I remember being angry with them because I wanted to go, to see David one last time, to be with my old friends. My brothers went and told me it was very sad. And when

I was fifteen, after Alex committed suicide, her body had been immediately cremated, with only a portrait and an urn representing her at the small memorial ceremony.

So I had never been to a traditional viewing until my classmate's. I remember the large crowd outside the tiny funeral home. We had all been given the opportunity to take time off from school to attend the funeral. As soon as I got close enough to see the casket, I began to feel intense anxiety build in my stomach and chest. I knew I was about to see her, and she would be dead. When I got close enough, I remember feeling overwhelmed with grief, and I began to sob uncontrollably.

She looked so pale and her eyes were closed, but she didn't look like she was sleeping. Her eyes were sewn shut, which was freaky looking. I went to the casket and stared at her, still sobbing. It was weird, because I didn't know her all that well, but I was a mess over it. I think all the emotions that I had over so much past stuff came up and spilled out all over the place.

But I quickly gained my composure. I didn't want anyone to think I was weak, so I wiped my eyes and walked out. I lit up a joint in the car and got stoned out of my mind. The thick white smoke exhaling from my mouth quickly eased the anxiety in my stomach, and my chest began to relax. I was safe again, high above the ground and floating over the world.

A COUPLE OF WEEKS LATER, another kid from my grade was killed while riding his bike in the woods. He ran into a wire, and it decapitated him. I didn't go to his viewing; I didn't know him well enough and felt like it would be wrong to go. But a bunch of us still got stoned in his honor. It seemed like the right thing to do.

A couple of weeks after that, a good friend of my brother's was shot and killed by a police officer in a freak misunderstanding near his house. He was a good kid and a really sweet person. He didn't really party like our crowd did. It was very sad and my brother was a mess. I went to his viewing. Again I had to see a dead body and the same feelings came up. I didn't allow myself to sob uncontrollably this time. I held it in. And again, as soon as I left, I got high as a kite to ease the pain.

Several months later, another student from my brother Brian's grade died in a DUI crash. The kid who died was very popular and cute. He wasn't really a big party person, never known for anything other than being a nice guy. Again I went to the viewing. It got to the point that I felt like I was going to a viewing every month. In reality, I guess I nearly was.

AROUND THIS TIME, another boy from our school, Lenny, was really close to Brian. Brian had just purchased a car from him, and Lenny had been at our house several times for parties. He was dating a girl who lived in our trailer park. Their relationship continued for a while, but at some point she broke up with him. Like most teenage girls, she just lost interest. Lenny was devastated. One day he came into our neighborhood and knocked on her door, which she and her mother came to answer. Moments after they opened the door, Lenny lifted a gun to his head and blew his brains out all over the aluminum siding of their trailer.

It was a rough time, and it only fueled my addiction more. I felt as though death was just everywhere, and it served as a great reason to keep self-medicating with drugs and alcohol. It got to the point where not only did the news of someone dying not surprise me, but I expected it. I had this impending sense of doom that right around the corner something else bad was going to happen. I was numb to it all, but deep down I carried with me this fear of what was going to come next. The dark pit in my stomach continued to grow, and I was truly empty inside. I was angry and bitter all the time, and it seemed that at every corner I turned, there was trauma. I was living with very limited supervision and seriously couldn't give a shit. My father was always at his girlfriend's house, my brothers were out doing the same thing I was, and my mother didn't care whether I was around or not, as long as I called for my daily dose of guilt.

12

Unhappy New Year's Eve

O N NEW YEAR'S EVE during my junior year, a bunch of us were hanging out at Richard's house. He and his neighbor were having a huge party, and all my usual friends were there, along with my brother Brian. I got very messed up that night. As usual, I drank more than my body could handle, and I smoked a lot of pot. Usually when I drank that much, I got sick, and this night was no different. After hours of partying and watching the New York City ball drop on TV at midnight, I was downstairs in Richard's house with a friend, Keith. We were smoking pot and listening to Pink Floyd. He and I had hung out a million times together and he used to date my best friend, plus he was the first guy I ever got high with, so I was very comfortable with him.

Nothing had ever happened between us before, but on this particular evening, he started hitting on me. When he kissed me, I returned the kiss. We made out for a while, but as we did, my head was spinning and my stomach started to churn. I got that ever-so-familiar feeling that I was going to be sick. The room began to seriously spin, and I told Keith I had to go upstairs because I was going to be sick. I remember stumbling up the stairs and finding my brother

Brian lying on the couch almost asleep. I was trying to find a place to lie down. There were bunk beds where Richard's children were already asleep, and the rest of the people were over at the neighbor's house still partying.

I stumbled over to the party and found Richard. I asked him if I could crash on his bed because I felt terrible. He said yes. The last thing I remember was falling onto Richard's bed fully clothed, and everything once again faded to black. I was severely intoxicated, and instead of puking like I usually did, I just blacked out.

THE NEXT MORNING, I woke up with my eyes sore and my head pounding. For a moment, I had no idea where I was. I slowly brought my head off the pillow and attempted to get my bearings when I realized that I had no shirt or bra on. I looked down, pulled the sheets off, and saw that I was totally naked. I began to freak out inside, trying to remember what the hell had happened the night before. I was alone in the bed. I felt between my legs and it was apparent that someone had had sex with me. I frantically looked around the room for my clothes. My head felt like a freight train had hit it and any quick movement hurt.

I found my clothes scattered all over the room and got dressed. I came out of the bedroom quietly to find Richard's two girls still asleep in their bunk beds and Richard lying in bed with his older daughter. I remember feeling very uncomfortable seeing him lying there so peacefully. Someone had violated me the night before, and I had no recollection of it at all. Brian was still passed out on the couch, and I went over to him and shook him awake. I asked him if anyone else had been in the house, and he said he didn't think so. I called my father and asked him to pick us up; I gave him directions and sat anxiously on the couch.

A few minutes later, Richard woke up. He stumbled out of bed and went into the kitchen. Brian said good morning to him, but Richard barely looked at either of us. He looked uncomfortable and avoided me completely. I sat on the couch in total silence for about ten minutes. All I could think was, "Oh my god, that bastard raped me while I was passed out." I was numb and totally emotionless. I couldn't believe that this was happening to me again! I couldn't comprehend how it was even possible. What was it with me? Why did guys treat me like this? Why did they think it was okay to do this?

My brother kept looking at me and asking what was wrong, and I said nothing. Richard just sat there looking down at the ground; he wouldn't say a word to me or look at me. I felt sick to my stomach and decided to go wait outside for my father. My brother joined me. He kept asking me what was wrong, and I couldn't say anything. I didn't even want to say what I knew in my head had happened. I didn't want it to be real, and I knew that as soon as I acknowledged it out loud, that would make it real and I would have to deal with it. My father arrived, and as we drove he kept questioning me, because he could tell something was wrong. I said, "I'm fine," and stared blankly out the window.

WE ARRIVED AT THE HOUSE and I went immediately to my room. I sat there for a while and the phone rang. It was my brother Jimmy. As soon as I heard his voice, I broke down and told him that I thought Richard had raped me the night before. At that time in my life, Jimmy and I were very close. I think we both realized how much we loved each other, and even though he picked on me growing up, he was getting older and realizing how much he loved me. After all, I was his only sister, and it was okay for him to make fun of me and torture me, but if someone else did, well, that was a whole other story. He became a source of protection for me, and if I had a problem, I knew I could turn to him and he would be there. I could hear the anger in Jimmy's voice. He asked me if I was sure, and I told him what had happened. He got off the phone after saying he was going over to Richard's house to find out what happened.

I told my father what had happened. He just shook his head. I could see utter exhaustion in his eyes, as if to say, "Not again." It seemed there was always something going on with our family, and it was never good. I felt so sorry for my father; we put him through hell and back. He said that we needed to go to the hospital, and so we did.

I had yet another rape kit done, my second in five years. Once again, I detached mentally and emotionally. My brain could not accept that this was happening again. "What is wrong with me?" was all I kept thinking. When we got home, Jimmy was in the kitchen looking very angry. He said he had gone to Richard's house and asked him what happened. Richard had told him we had consensual sex. Jimmy then beat him up pretty badly. Keith told Jimmy that I had been very drunk and making out with him in the basement—as though that were reason enough to believe that I would have then gone upstairs and had sex willingly with Richard. My brother looked me dead in the eyes and asked, "Are you sure he raped you?" I looked right back and told him again the entire story. Yes, I remembered kissing Keith, but I also stopped because I was so drunk and felt sick, and the last thing I remembered was hitting the bed and blacking out. I didn't remember a thing, so how could I have had sex without giving consent? My brother just nodded and believed me, which felt good.

THE DAYS AND WEEKS THAT CAME NEXT were horrible as word got out to all our mutual friends. My friends supported me, except for Richard's cousin; she was very upset and didn't know what to believe. I think more than anything she just didn't want to believe it. Richard's house had become a safe haven for all of us, and he had been a main supplier of our alcohol and drugs. I think people were more upset by the fact that they were losing their dealer and a safe place to party.

The police launched an investigation, and when they began a background check on Richard, they found a long history of criminal behavior. As the case progressed, some other people came forward making allegations against Richard.

My father took care of the case and hired an attorney. I remember that I did not want to have to go to a hearing; I couldn't take going through all that again. I was so numb and emotionless at that point that I wanted to die. Richard took a plea bargain and was sentenced to several years in prison. I was relieved that he took ownership of his actions and that I didn't have to go to court. I think he may have served two years or something ridiculous like that. I don't know exactly how much time, but I do remember that years later, while I was working at a travel agency in Allentown, I bumped into him in the lobby of the building where I worked. I think he was in a work-release program at the time. I just froze when I saw him. He was cleaning the floors of the building. He paused when he noticed me looking at him in shock, and then he looked back toward the floor he was cleaning. I never saw or heard of him again after that.

AS THE NEW YEAR BEGAN, I pushed the whole event deep down and never spoke of it again. I didn't want anyone talking about it or asking me questions. I wanted to pretend it never happened. I had reached a point where I was in such utter disbelief that I felt almost like I deserved it. I must have been doing something to attract these bad things in my life. I couldn't figure out what it could have been. Was I simply a bad person?

My father started to say that it was my drinking, and I got defensive. There was no way that drinking was causing these problems. Drinking and doing drugs were my only solace at this point. I saw no connection between the bad things that happened and my abuse. I needed drugs and alcohol just to cope with the everyday reality of my life. The thought of them being the cause of my troubles was too much for me to grasp, so I blew it off and got high to deal with the pain.

13

Addicted Before Exhaling

MY BROTHER JIMMY had a very violent temper when he drank. One night he and a bunch of his friends were up in Potter County hunting all day and drinking all night. They were driving around in a pickup truck that happened to have some apples in the back. They were hammered, and Jimmy and some other guys in the back of the truck began throwing the apples. Apparently one of the apples hit a vehicle behind them, smashing into the windshield and hurting the woman in the car badly. The woman, it turned out, was the wife of the commissioner of Potter County, and in a small town, this was huge news.

Jimmy got arrested and took the rap for the others in the car. He was the kind of person who, no matter what his involvement was, would never rat out his friends. So he took all the blame and ended up spending a year in the Potter County jail. It was terrible; they treated him like shit there. I remember traveling four hours to visit him. When we arrived, we had to visit behind a steel door that had one little hole in the top. I could barely see his whole face. I hated the people in that county for making my brother into some kind of huge criminal. The woman had some damage to her face but overall was okay. I am not excusing what he did, but I think it is incredible the way society responds to a crime when the victim is well known, compared with all the everyday people who are victimized and given no special treatment. He was painted in the media as a monster. One headline read, "Storm Hits Potter County." It was sensationalized and exaggerated. My brother was not a monster; he had a good heart but was misguided. We all were. He just wore his anger on his sleeve and hurt others with it. I turned my anger in on myself. Everyone deals with not dealing with things in their own way.

WITH JIMMY IN PRISON AND MY DAD always sleeping over at Pat's house, Brian and I threw huge parties at the house in the trailer park. Dad would come home the next day and always find something that led him to believe we had had a party the night before. He was quite the detective, and even though we thought we had cleaned everything up, he would find something. One day he came home after I thought I had done a stellar job cleaning the entire house, only to find that I missed the fact that it had snowed that night and there were footprints all over the front and back of the house. My father followed several tracks around to the shed that led to a pile of vomit from one of my friends the night before.

After that day, he made Brian and me move to Allentown to live with him and Pat. This was fine with me, because I had my own bedroom and bathroom in her basement. Her house was also much closer to my friends' houses. When I was home, which at this point was almost never, I hid down in my basement bedroom. My dad would get pissed, off but there was nothing he could do; he had no real control over me.

DURING MY JUNIOR YEAR OF HIGH SCHOOL, I began hanging out with this girl, Amanda, who was a senior. We partied together and I stayed over at her house a lot. She lived in a huge house up on a hill in the middle of nowhere, with beautiful horses on several acres of land. I envied her, her wealth, and her clothes. She met this guy, Ron, who was much older than she, and they began dating. One night while I was hanging out with them, we went over to his friend Doug's house. We had been smoking pot and drinking, and when we arrived, we went into Doug's bedroom and continued to party. Doug was cute, and I took a liking to him right away. He lived with his father, who was rarely home, and even when he was, he just sat downstairs in front of the television and left us alone to do whatever we wanted upstairs.

While we sat there talking, Doug took out a plastic bag with white powder in it. I knew right away that it was cocaine. I had seen it in movies such as *Less Than Zero*, and I remembered how glamorous Jami Gertz's character looked sniffing it up her nose. I had never done it before but was always fascinated by what I saw in movies about it. Doug took a plate from under his chair and swiftly cut the white powder into four bulky lines next to each other. He picked up a $20 bill and rolled it up like a cigarette. He placed it up his nostril and lifted the plate to his face. I watched him quickly snort one of the fat white lines of powder up his nose. He made a funny noise and passed the plate to me along with the rolled-up bill. I carefully took it from his hand and stared at the sparkling white powder laid out before me. I nervously picked up the bill. I didn't want Doug to know this was my first time, so I tried to be cool and pretend I had done this a million times before. I inserted the bill into my nose. It felt wet and cold. I raised the plate up to my face, placed the bill in front of the pile of cocaine, and slowly began to snort it up my right nostril. I immediately felt a tingling sensation that ran up my nose and down my spine. It made the hairs on my neck and arms stand up. I sniffed real hard to make sure I got it all up my nose as I passed the plate to Amanda.

Within minutes, I began to feel a drip down my throat that was bitter as hell as it hit the back of my mouth. My head began to feel heavy and a rush of adrenaline filled me. I felt alive and wide awake all of a sudden. The slight buzz I had going on from the beer and pot went away. I felt good, all my worries and uneasy feelings went away, and I began chatting away like I had known Doug all my life. We talked for hours and hours while he continued to cut lines and pass them around. I didn't leave his house until very late that night.

Amanda and I got to her house around 3 A.M., and we had to be at school the next day. I remember lying on her bed knowing we had to be up in less than three hours. I couldn't sleep. I was jacked up, and my mind was spinning out of control. I finally fell asleep about a half hour before the alarm went off. I remember feeling like shit all day and heading to the nurse's office during second period. Amanda met me there, and we decided to skip the rest of the day and go over to Doug's. This began my relationship with Doug. He was a drug dealer at the time, dealing small amounts of pot and cocaine locally. I began spending every night at his house.

I WAS BASICALLY LIVING AT DOUG'S, and he was still dealing drugs and making lots of money. He started smoking crack around this time. This really freaked me out. I would watch him and his friend get all fucked up on this stuff, and I swore I wouldn't do it. It scared me. I would sit and do lines of cocaine while they smoked this weird stuff that looked like little rocks and then acted all paranoid. They would get quiet and their eyes would change, turning all glossy with huge pupils. Doug and his friends looked scary and acted like idiots. I hated when Doug smoked, because he acted so weird, and I couldn't talk to him.

I was always looking for something to numb my pain, and thus far drinking and smoking dope had worked. But doing coke gave me something that alcohol and drugs did not, which was an illusion of control. When I started doing cocaine, I realized that I could drink as much as I wanted as long as I did a couple of lines every hour or so. It was almost like the coke would sober me up enough to allow me to drink more. I loved this effect, because it removed the blackout factor for me. As long as I was doing coke, I didn't have as many nights in which I didn't remember anything. Cocaine became my drinking crutch; it got to the point where I couldn't go out and drink without doing coke. See, for me it was always about the alcohol, and now I had found a tool that would enable me to drink all night and not black out.

From that time forward, alcohol and cocaine went hand in hand for me. This worked out rather well, as all my friends at this time were doing coke. And since my boyfriend was selling it, I had access to it all the time.

ONE NIGHT I WAS SITTING AT DOUG'S when the phone rang. Doug came in, handed me the phone, and said it was my dad. My father hated that I stayed at Doug's all the time, but he learned to accept it. I think it was easier for him because he and Pat didn't have to see how I was really living. He didn't sound good, and I immediately knew something was wrong. He told me that my Uncle Ben had called and said that Thomas was dead.

Thomas had a lot of problems and was really struggling, just like me. When he was younger, he and a friend of his were playing behind a shopping center near a trash compactor. His friend climbed on top of the trash compactor, slipped, and fell into it. The trash compactor was turned on, and Thomas watched helplessly as his friend was eaten alive by it. The incident left him scarred, and he was never really the same after that. He would visit Jimmy over the years, and they would go party together, but after my parents' divorce, we didn't visit like we had when I was little.

I froze as Dad gave me the details of what appeared to be a suicide, which didn't surprise me considering Thomas's problems. Apparently he had gone to Las Vegas by himself and was found in his hotel room in the hot tub. The details were sketchy, to say the least. We didn't know really whether he died of a drug overdose, killed himself, or got drunk, passed out, and died from the heat.

The latter was the story my aunt and uncle went with, as I think it was too painful for them to conceive of anything else. Uncle Ben had to fly out to Vegas to identify his body, which apparently was in bad shape from being in the hot tub for a couple of days. We went to the funeral, and it was a closed casket. Attending the funeral was awful, and I was not doing well. This was the first time a person in my extended "family" had died. I didn't know how to handle it and, of course, our family barely talked about it. A month to the day after Thomas died, my uncle died of a heart attack while shoveling snow. I decided not to go to the funeral; I couldn't bear to face my aunt and cousin. I couldn't imagine the pain they must have been going through at that time. I was numb and in shock. I was so sick of people dying; I couldn't make any sense of it.

DOUG AND I WERE OUT AT A PARTY one night, and I was getting out-of-hand drunk, which was my usual mode. I didn't want to feel at all. We were doing coke and needed more, so we went back to his house, where his stash was. When we got there, he looked at me and asked if I wouldn't mind if he smoked a little before we went back to the party. I didn't care; I didn't care about anything at that point. I watched him pull out a bag of coke and set it on the table; he then took out a box of baking soda and other items. I watched with fascination as the white crystals of the baking soda hit the soft white powder of the coke and he prepared the mixture like a trained chemist. Soon, a solid, rock-like matter formed. This was crack.

I was amazed at how easy it was for Doug to turn the powder into what I knew was crack cocaine. I had never really watched what he and his friends were doing, because I wanted no part of it. But this night, I continued to watch as he pulled a Budweiser can out from under his bed. It was all crushed and had holes. He put some ashes from the ashtray onto the little holes. I asked him what he was doing and he said that this was what you smoke crack out of. Then he looked at me and said, "Do you want a hit?" I stared at him for a moment; I was scared but so totally wanted something to take the immense pain away. After Thomas and my uncle died, I was just barely getting by, and alcohol and regular coke weren't really numbing the pain like they used to. I nodded yes and he handed me the can. He then gave me instructions for what I was supposed to do.

I lifted the can to my mouth and immediately smelled stale beer and cigarettes. I placed my finger over one of the holes, and Doug nodded at me to see if I was ready. I very gently nodded my head. He flicked a flame over the rock. I heard a sizzling noise and immediately began to inhale as hard as I could. A rush of bittersweet smoke filled my mouth and lungs; I let go of the hole, and another quick rush of smoke entered my body. I held it and held it as my head began to feel light as a feather. Doug motioned for me to exhale, and as I did a small smile crept to my face, and I knew I had just found what I had been looking for. It instantly made me feel good, light, and carefree. All the emptiness in my stomach, the big, black, tight hole in the pit of my stomach, went away. This drug did everything I had always wanted alcohol and other drugs to do—it took away all the pain and left me feeling numb and peaceful. I immediately wanted more. In that instant, crack became my best friend. I was addicted before I even exhaled.

14

Credits and Demerits

B ECAUSE OF CONSTANTLY SKIPPING SCHOOL, I ended up failing several grades: first seventh grade, then ninth, and eventually eleventh. Each time I made sure to go to summer school and do what I needed to do, because there was no way I was going to repeat a grade. The embarrassment and thought of staying back in school and how that would look to my friends would be just enough to spur me into action to at least do the minimum requirements to pass the course or the grade.

After ninth grade, my friend Tim also failed and had to go to summer school, so his mother and my dad worked out a schedule to drive us each day. Neither of us had a driver's license yet.

I was going out every night but still managed to make it to summer school—even if it meant crawling into class wearing the same outfit I wore to the previous night's party. I was learning how far I could push my limits. I didn't require a lot of sleep, so staying up all night partying till dawn and then going to class didn't faze me.

Tim was a really sweet guy. He and I studied together and hung out a little bit that summer. He didn't really run with my crowd, but I always had an ability to run with any of the other crowds in school. I was like a chameleon; I could blend into whatever my surroundings were and fit in with any crowd. I didn't have any real sense of self; I had no true identity at this point and just became whatever I thought I should be in any given moment, whatever I thought people wanted me to be. Because of this, I was friends with all types of people in high school and could easily adapt to any social setting.

A year after Tim and I went to summer school, he got his license and bought a motorcycle. One night after a party, he was driving down the highway, crashed his bike, and was killed. He died instantly. Yet another viewing and funeral to attend. Another face gone, and another space to add to my black pit.

DURING JUNIOR YEAR, I was skipping school even more, because I would be up all night doing lines of coke with Doug and couldn't wake up for class the next day. I didn't fail classes because I was stupid. In fact, I was very intelligent, and all my teachers would say, "She is such a bright child; if only she would apply herself." The thing was, I didn't care. I was too busy partying to be bothered with school. I saw no value in it, and I wanted to escape everything, so skipping school and getting high became my everyday existence. Which then, obviously, led me to failing many classes. And eleventh grade. Which led to summer school again before my senior year.

Even after passing my summer-school classes, though, during my senior year it became evident that I would not have enough credits to graduate. I wanted desperately to graduate. Even though I didn't care about school and acted tough, I still knew deep down that I needed a diploma, and it was important to me to get it. I had watched Brian quit school in eleventh grade and thought he was such an idiot for doing so. Now he had to get his GED and struggle to find a good job. He ended up working in a factory downtown. That would not be me.

So I met with my guidance counselor to find out what I would have to do to graduate on time. I learned that even if I passed all my senior classes, technically I wouldn't have enough credits to graduate. If I wanted to graduate on time with my class, I would have to find a way to get more credits completed during my senior year.

So I enrolled at Northampton Community College and took nine credits in the evenings. I kind of liked going to the community college; it made me feel smart to be in those classes with older kids. I actually went to class and passed each one, which supplemented the classes I failed that year and gave me enough credits to graduate that spring.

No one in my family had ever gone to college, and it was not something my parents instilled in me as being important; they would just be happy if I graduated high school. My father was able to make a lot of money by working in sales, so he never saw the value of college. And seeing how badly I fucked up high school, he was not about to put any resources toward a college education for me.

Now I had the credits to graduate. What I didn't realize was how many demerits I had from skipping school and getting in trouble. The school had made a new policy that anyone with more than fifty demerits could not attend graduation. Well, I had 100 demerits from skipping eighty-two days of school. There are only something like 185 days in a school year, so this was pretty bad.

I was told that because of my demerits I could not attend my own graduation ceremony. While everyone else woke up on graduation day and got all dressed up and went to the ceremony, I got drunk instead and went to all the parties.

I REMEMBER GOING TO THE SCHOOL a couple of days later to pick up my diploma, and the woman working there handed me my cap and gown. I looked at the lady with hatred. "What the fuck am I supposed to do with this?" I asked. It felt like a kick in the stomach.

I took the cap and gown home and went downstairs to my bedroom. I slipped on the white gown and placed the cap on my head. I tried to think of what it would have been like to be at graduation. I started to get upset, so I tore them off and stuck them in my closet, where they stayed for years.

A couple of days later, I was over at my friend Jessica's house. She was watching a videotape her parents had taken of the graduation ceremony, and I sat and watched as all my friends walked up on stage to receive their diplomas. I was so angry at the school for not letting me attend what should have been a huge rite of passage for me. I was angry at myself for fucking up and not being able to go.

Jessica had given me a program to take home, and I looked through it and saw that my name was listed. I felt bad that my parents didn't get to go to my graduation either. It's not that my mother would have driven up for the event, since she didn't even drive up to my house just to see me or to pick me up when I needed a ride to work, but I thought it would have been nice for my father. They really didn't seem to care much, though. I think everyone was just relieved that I had made it and got my diploma.

I REMEMBER MY OLDEST BROTHER JIMMY had a huge graduation party. All his friends came, and he had a lot of presents. Since Brian had quit school and never graduated, there was no party for him. And I didn't have a party or anything and didn't receive any presents. There was no celebration of this event. It was a non-event in my house. I was too bad to have a party, I guess.

I was pissed, and it just added to the bundle of feelings that I pushed aside and never dealt with. I was still dating Doug at this time and partying a lot. I smoked pot daily, drank almost every night, and was doing a lot of cocaine with Doug and all my friends. Now I found myself thrust into the "real" world and needing to find a job.

SHORTLY AFTER GRADUATION, I got this great job at a life insurance company, but there was one catch: After my probationary period, I had to pass a drug test before they would hire me permanently. I was told on a Friday that my drug test was scheduled for Monday. I panicked, knowing that I had smoked pot a couple of days earlier. Doug gave me some goldenseal, an herb, and said as long as I took it, my urine should run clean. So all I had to do was get through the weekend without doing any more drugs and take the test on Monday, and I was in the clear.

By nine that night, Doug and his friends were at the house getting high. At first I kept saying no when they offered drugs to me. I knew I had to take this test, and I wanted to keep this job. It was a good job, and I had done really well there for my first month or two—at least when I showed up. I processed insurance claims and did a lot of data entry and phone calling, but it offered a decent salary with good benefits. Plus it was one of those companies where you could make a nice career out of the work and earn a good pension. But the temptation was too strong.

After an hour of saying no, I broke down, got high, and ended up awake till the birds were chirping.

By Sunday I had done enough drugs to piss out a line of fresh cocaine into a cup, and I knew I was screwed. I kept asking people for ideas about what I could use to help me pass the test. Someone told me that drinking vinegar would clean out my system. Another told me that if I took bladder-infection medication, it would do the same. So I filled a twenty-four-ounce squeeze bottle full of ice and poured an entire bottle of white vinegar over the ice. I drank the entire thing, gagging the whole time. I kept feeling bile rising in my throat, but I just held my nose and drank it as fast as I could. I eventually threw up, and it was totally disgusting. Then I took a couple of my friend's bladder-infection pills, the ones that make your urine turn all kinds of funky bright colors, like red and orange, while they work the infection out of you.

I went into work on Monday with a sore throat from puking and a severe hangover from the weekend's partying. And when they handed me a cup, I peed bright orange! Needless to say, I failed the drug test and was fired the next day.

15

Evolving Relationships

WHEN I FOUND OUT THAT MY MOTHER had been diagnosed with breast cancer, I remember not feeling anything about it. I just took it in as I did all the other random pieces of information that passed by and through me on any given day. This was no different. I was sad and, I guess, scared, but I never had a good enough connection to these feelings to really know what they were in their actual state. I blocked emotions out of my mind like everything else and went about my business.

My mother was freaking out and of course planning her funeral in the melodramatic way that she dealt with everything in her life. Deep down, a part of me was genuinely scared of what could happen to her. She told us that she had to have surgery to have one of her breasts removed. I went to the hospital with my brothers and my father on the day of the surgery and watched the doctors wheel her into the surgical unit. She came out of it fine, and they claimed to have removed all the cancer in her body. She emerged from the surgery cancer-free but missing her right breast.

I knew this had to have been very traumatic for her. I could not even imagine having to lose one of my breasts. She dealt with it rather well. My mother had a great sense of humor, just like the rest of our family—after all, humor was how we dealt and how we communicated. When she wasn't being completely melodramatic about everything, she was quite fun and funny. Over the months when I would go to her place to visit, she would show me her fake boob and make a joke of it. Once, she told me how she was on a date and the guy she was kissing was feeling her up for a while before he realized it was her fake boob. I laughed, not particularly because it was funny, but more because I knew she needed to make light of it.

These conversations became the type of dialogue she and I would have. We didn't have mother-daughter talks; she never really commented on or cared about what was really happening in my life the way a mother should. She started treating me more like a friend than a daughter anyway, so telling me stories about hooking up with guys became commonplace.

We had such a fucked-up relationship. It was like a dangerous roller coaster that I had to keep riding. It was as though the pain I felt every time I hung up the phone with her was a drug I couldn't live without. No matter how much she made me feel like shit, I would call the next day for my daily dose of judgment and disappointment.

By this time, Doug and I had briefly tried living together in an apartment, but he was out of hand with the drug use, even more so than I was. He would disappear and show up a day later. While I was at work, he would have huge crack parties at our apartment, and when I came home, it would be trashed. I was sick of it and told him one night that I was going to break up with him. I don't know if I was pissed because he was partying while I had to work or if I was just done with the relationship, period. But I used the drugs as an excuse for breaking up with him either way. He left the house that night, out to party, I was sure. I left him a note on the counter saying that I was serious and that the relationship was over, and I went to sleep that night.

I AWOKE TO HIM ON TOP OF ME with his hands around my throat, strangling me. I was startled and quickly felt around for something to grab. I managed to wiggle and reach over to grab a Red Rover vacuum that was sitting near my bed. I promptly and swiftly swung it up and hit him over the head with it. He fell to the side and let go of me. He was hammered, and there was a crazy look in his eyes. I ran out of the house, hopped in my car, and drove to a friend's house. I called him and told him to pack his shit and get out.

The next day when I came back to the apartment, he was moving out and very apologetic about what he had done. He was not a violent person; the drugs had made him do it. I wasn't hearing any of it. In my mind the relationship was over. He moved out and that was the last I heard from him.

I asked a friend of mine to move in, because I didn't want to lose the apartment. I continued to drink and do drugs as I had been, going from party to party with my friends and having no real emotion or meaning in my life. I had been doing cocaine on an almost daily basis, and things were really beginning to spin out of control. I got fired from a factory job for not coming in to work, I was throwing crazy parties in my apartment, and my new roommate was starting to get fed up with me rolling in at all hours of the night or having people over until the wee hours of the morning. I was going to bars all the time even though I wasn't close to twenty-one. I had a fake ID, as most of my friends did. And if that didn't work, I would flirt with the door man and get in.

IN FACT, I'D BEGUN GOING TO BARS by the time I was fifteen, when I was working at the roach-infested restaurant. I held a second job then, too, at a movie theater in Easton, mainly as an excuse to be closer to my mother in hopes of actually spending quality time with her. Sometimes I would stay over at my mother's apartment and crash on her couch, but that was the exception. Most of the time, my father ended up picking me up and taking me to work. Or I relied on my friends who had driver's licenses by this time.

While working at the theater, I began casually dating my twenty-one-year-old manager. Since he was of age, he took me to nice restaurants and ordered wine for us with dinner. I never once got questioned or carded.

With my confidence built up from that, we went to various bars around Easton and Allentown. I felt at home in a bar; it was dark and dreary, kind of like me, so it suited me well. In bars, there was an overflowing amount of alcohol, cigarette machines, and music blaring from jukeboxes. I loved it.

I always got in without a question. Granted, I was dressing older, and certainly acting older than fifteen. And if a bouncer would start to question me or look inquisitively at me, I would just flash a big smile and flirt my way onto my bar seat.

It worked every time—until I started trying to get into some of the bigger clubs. One night, I faced rejection at the door of a dance club because I didn't have any ID card at all. I left feeling pissed off that I couldn't get in and embarrassed that I had to walk past the line of card-carrying people waiting to get in who had just witnessed my rejection.

It was then that I cooked up a little plan to ensure my bar seat would always be available.

In the 1990s, drivers' licenses were not as sophisticated as they are today. A clear plastic sheath covered the front of the card that showed all your relevant information, such as your picture, date of birth, and eye color. There were no holograms or blaring green lettering that read "Under 21 until" the way there are now. I had heard from older kids at school about altering IDs.

Being the ever-resourceful gal that I was, I noticed that if I picked a little at the corner of my ID, the clear plastic sheath would lift off the license, exposing the vital information. I found an eraser and erased the year of my birthday. To my delight, it came off without too much effort. I sharpened the pencil as pointy as I could get it and wrote in a date that made me of legal age to drink. I then grabbed the iron from my dad's room, put a towel over the ID as to not burn the plastic right off, and gently ironed over the towel enough to heat up the plastic until it re-adhered itself to the ID. Voilà—I was twenty-one!

I showed some of my friends how I did it, and we did their IDs, too. Then it was time for the big test. My friends and I went back to the club where I had been rejected—this time with our faked IDs in hand. One by one, we handed over our IDs with big flirty grins, and one by one, we were let into the club. I started venturing out to bars all over town after that.

Word got out about my new skill, and I began a little business charging people $25 per license. So when

I actually turned twenty-one years later, the whole rite of passage to enter a bar legally was nothing to me. I had been doing it for more than five years already.

EVENTUALLY MY FRIEND MOVED OUT of the apartment Doug and I had shared, leaving me with no choice but to call my dad and Pat, who had become my stepmother since they had married that year. They came to the apartment and cleaned it out, which was a job and a half because it was disgusting. I hadn't been taking care of it; I was just partying. They let me move back into the basement of their house.

My stepmom, Pat, was different, more nurturing and loving than the family I'd grown up with—all males and my mother and grandmother, who were certainly not good role models. She took the time to talk to me and ask questions, and she hugged me for no reason at all, like it was just natural. My own mother never did that. For someone who never had children, Pat certainly knew what a child needed, and she gave that to me. It was a stability that I cannot even begin to explain.

She added structure to my life. For the first time since my parents divorced, we had family dinners. When I would come home, she and my father would be in the kitchen making dinner, and we would sit down together and eat like a real family. I hadn't had that since I was fourteen or so. On our birthdays, both my brothers' included, she would make a big deal out of them, buying birthday plates with matching napkins and making us a nice dinner of our personal favorite foods and cake. It was the whole nine yards. And we would sit around the table and laugh and really enjoy each other's company. On holidays, she made sure all three of us were there for dinner, and even though we would sometimes be horribly hungover or still drunk from the night before, we came to the table when called and we ate. She came into my room and made my bed when I didn't. She also picked up my laundry. I would come home and find it all clean and folded neatly on my bed.

At first I didn't know how to take her, because all her niceties and attention were so foreign, but eventually I grew to enjoy it and felt good knowing that she cared about me. In many ways I believe Pat was a core reason why I am still alive today. Had my father not met her and had she not come into our lives, I have no idea where I would be. Unfortunately, at this time I was too far into my addiction for her actions to have a real impact on mine. Yet she did plant a seed of normalcy or hope in me that had not been there in a long time. Again, I was too deep into my addiction to really grasp it all, so I kind of just blew it off and kept using.

I still partied hard and stayed out late or never came home. I kept getting these really great jobs, and then I would lose them months later because I could not get up and go to work after partying all night. I would still be out until seven or eight in the morning—the time when everyone else was getting ready for work.

16

Crying in a Clinic

I STARTED QUASI-DATING THIS GUY who hung around
the bar I frequented. Maybe *dating* isn't the word, really;
we began sleeping together. It was pretty casual, and
I didn't have much interest in him at all, but he always
seemed to have lots of drugs, which suited me just fine.
We would get together and party and then end up in bed
together. He was a real loser who worked at the carnival
and traveled most of the year. I happened upon him during
his downtime, lucky me. He had a child on the way with a
previous fling, and I should have known better than to get
involved with him, but really, I simply didn't care. He was
decent company and had good dope.

I had just been hired at a day-care center and was
enjoying working there. They started me working in the
infant room, which I totally loved. I love babies, love being
around children. One day, one of my co-workers went to
McDonald's for lunch and brought back a Big Mac and
fries. I had been a near-vegetarian nearly all my life. I ate
chicken occasionally, but I had never had beef, not for any
animal-rights reasons, just because I thought it was totally
disgusting. On this particular day, though, the minute
my co-worker walked in with her bag of beef, my nostrils

flared. The smell was intoxicating, and suddenly I began to crave meat in a way that I never had. I wanted the Big Mac she was eating more than anything in the world. It was very odd.

By the end of the day, I had fantasized about this freaking burger to the point of insanity. I found myself sitting in the drive-through at McDonald's ordering a Big Mac and fries. I felt so weird; I had never craved anything like this in my life. Why now? I felt incredibly guilty for some reason, so I parked in an empty space by the drive-through and wolfed down the burger so fast that I almost puked. I had never tasted anything so incredible in my life. I knew something was wrong with me. And then it hit me. I immediately went to the drugstore and purchased a pregnancy test.

I WAS STILL LIVING WITH MY PARENTS, Dad and Pat, at the time. When I came home, I hid the drugstore bag under my jacket and went straight downstairs to my bedroom. I locked the door behind me, pulled the test out of the bag, and stared at it for the longest time. The instructions said to use it first thing in the morning. The next day was Saturday, so I decided to put it away and use it in the morning as directed. I went out that night and got vividly hammered as usual, but I didn't mutter a word about my suspicions to anyone. I came home earlier than usual, around 4 A.M. I woke up the next day, grabbed the test out of my underwear drawer, where I had stashed it the night before, and went into the bathroom. I was so nervous. I knew something was off. The Big Mac tipped me off that something was fucked up. There was no sensible reason why I would have craved a hamburger in that way when I had never eaten one before.

I sat on the toilet and unwrapped the stick that held my fate. My hands shook as I placed it under myself and peed on it. I set it on the sink and finished going to the bathroom. Before I could stand up, the little indicator window had lit up like a Christmas tree with a big plus sign. Fuck, I was pregnant. I knew I was before I even looked at the stick. I had this terrible feeling, and the whole Big Mac craving pretty much gave it away. I sat on the toilet for a long time just staring at the plus sign wondering what the hell I was going to do.

I had always fantasized about being pregnant. I have always been fascinated by pregnant women; I think they are incredibly beautiful and sexy. Many of my friends already had children by this time, and I wondered what it would be like.

I finally got off the toilet and went upstairs where my dad and Pat were hanging out. I sat at the kitchen table and stared off into space. I just kept thinking, I am nineteen and not ready for any of this. Nor do I want to have a baby with this fucking loser I have been sleeping with. Shit—what was I going to do? My dad looked at me and asked what was wrong. I simply burst into tears. The thought of telling them this killed me. The thought of having to disappoint them with more bad news just tore me up. All I ever did was disappoint them with my actions.

I looked at my dad and stepmother and simply said, "I'm pregnant." My father got angry and sat down and looked at me. All I remember was my father bitching, my stepmother listening, and me crying. After about an hour of this, we collectively decided that I would not have the baby. I would have an abortion.

I called my mother to inform her and got exactly what I expected from her, which was guilt and shame with a side of painful judgment. Typical.

I spent the night lying in bed staring at the ceiling, wondering what it would be like to have a child and be a mother. As I rubbed my belly in the same loving fashion I had seen so many pregnant women do, I wondered whether I would be a good mother. I decided I would never be like my mother; I would never judge my child or verbally abuse my child the way my mother did to me. I would love my children unconditionally and tell them each and every day how wonderful they were. I would shower my children with love so they never doubted for one minute whether my love was true. My children would never have to wonder whether they were good enough for my love, the way I did with my mother.

THE NEXT DAY MY FATHER AND I made an appointment for an abortion at a local clinic. It would probably seem odd to most people that my father was the one taking me, but this was par for the course. My father was the one who was always there, took me wherever I needed to go, and provided for me for my whole life. My mother didn't want to go; she made some excuse about not being able to get off work. It made sense to have my father take me. He was the only person I could rely on.

My stepmother was starting to become one of those people, too, which was a nice feeling. She and I had a great talk the day before I went for my abortion. She disclosed some things to me that really encouraged me. She was such a kindhearted, loving person. I am so grateful to have her in my life. My father had made a good choice this time. She showed me a form of unconditional love that I should have received from my birth mother—truly it was the first unconditional love that I had ever received. It was nice to finally have a stable female role model in my life.

MY FATHER AND I PULLED UP TO THE CLINIC in the early morning hours. I was nervous; I had no idea what to expect. As we parked the car, I saw a stream of people with signs standing outside the front door. I had no idea who they were or what they were doing there. We both walked slowly toward the door, and as we approached, we realized these people were not a Welcome Wagon for young women. Rather, they were there to protest abortion and try to change people's minds. They began quoting scripture and yelling obscenities as we walked past them. They held signs that read "Murder" and showed pictures of bloody babies. Just as when Kristen's dad found us dancing, I was again being told in the name of Christ that I was going to hell. Since that day he chased me out of their house, I had really started to resent these Christian people. I must say, for people who purport to be loving and godlike, these Christian types I had met were very mean. My experience with them thus far had been very negative. If they were trying to save me, why were they yelling at me? If God is all forgiving and loving, why was I being told I was going to hell? None of it made sense to me, and it left me knowing that I would never want to be a Christian. Had these people nothing better to do than stand outside a clinic and yell at other people in the name of Christ? Somehow, I thought that if Jesus were here, he would not be standing in line with these psychos. Something told me he would have better things to do.

WE MADE IT INSIDE THE CLINIC and checked in for my appointment. I sat, pretending to read a magazine, as I waited for them to call my name. My father tried to make small talk in that offbeat comedic way he always did when he was uncomfortable. He would make observational jokes about the people in the waiting room, like, "Who slept with that woman and got her pregnant?" finding irony in everything he saw. He called the protestors "assholes with nothing better to do." I played along and made small talk back. I loved him for being there with me. He was such a good man.

In the middle of our small talk, a nurse came out and called my name. I looked up at my father nervously and smiled slightly. There was a deep sadness in his eyes as they connected with my eyes, which held the same sadness. I said, "I love you," and walked toward the door.

The nurse began to explain the procedure to me as I undressed and got into a gown. I was so nervous and felt incredibly sick to my stomach. I sat up on the table and stared at the vacuum-like machine that would be sucking the life out of me, literally. I was about six weeks pregnant. The doctor and nurse did an ultrasound, and as I looked at the screen, I saw no visible heartbeat and heard no sounds. I asked them where the baby was, and the nurse pointed to a small, almost nonexistent, blur on the screen. It was like nothing. It made me feel better about what I was about to do. I don't know how I would have handled seeing an actual heart beating or any sign of life. I am not sure I would have been able to go through with it if that had been the case.

The nurse was not very friendly. I attempted to make the same nervous comedic small talk with her that my father had made with me, but she wasn't into talking. She was cold with a distance in her eyes that was slightly scary. As the doctor explained the procedure, I had to lie down on the table. He said that I would hear a suction sound and feel some pressure in my vaginal area. He said it would be over in minutes. I felt the cold metal as he placed the speculum inside me. The nurse took my hand in a very uncaring, routine manner. As the machine came on, all I could hear was a loud suction noise. It sounded like the large vacuum at a car wash.

As the doctor inserted the machine into me, I slowly began to detach. I floated above myself and found a safe holding pattern. I could feel the pressure and the coldness and hear the noise in the background, but I was not totally present. I was above, floating in the safe zone I had created for myself when I was younger. I tried to think about happy things but couldn't find any memories to grasp on to, so I thought about the past couple of years of my life. I began to feel incredibly sad, a feeling I did not associate well with at all. I felt overwhelmed by this sadness that crept out of my soul to the surface, and tears began to spill from my eyes. I rarely cried, and as this happened I got very angry with myself.

The nurse who was holding my hand looked at me with this angry look in her eyes and asked me in a very nasty tone why I was crying. It was almost accusatory, the way she blurted it out. As if I had no right to be upset because I was here having an abortion. As if my heart should have been as numb and distant as her eyes. I looked at her and stopped crying immediately.

I LEFT THE CLINIC THAT DAY and never really looked back. I don't think about the whole thing very often. I never sit and ponder what would have been or what my child would look like or be like. I cannot even conceive in my mind that I was ever really carrying an actual child. My pregnancy was so early on that I didn't even see anything on the screen, and I never heard a heartbeat. It was never really real to me. I think it was meant to be that way.

17

Opportunity in Maryland

AFTER HAVING THE ABORTION, I had no real future plans and had been fired from yet another job, this time at the day-care center where I had been working. I didn't care, because after what I had just been through, I had no desire to be around infants. I was still going out almost every night and hitting the bars hard. I had found a group of much older friends who were into smoking crack, and I was hanging out with them. My brothers were also a part of this crowd—we seemed to maintain the same group of friends as we each progressed through our individual addictions. Many of my high school friends were also getting heavy into coke and smoking crack at this time, too.

I was quickly getting to know many dealers in our town. My ex-boyfriend Doug had introduced me to some, and later I met others through some friends at the bars where I was hanging out. I put myself in many dangerous situations, like being at a dealer's house while people were measuring more grams of cocaine than I could imagine onto large scales and packaging them for sale. In one room, the pool table piled with pounds of pot in large sealed blocks was just waiting for a pick. Who knows how much time I would have done if the police would have come in at any of those times.

At this point I had a couple of main dealers I went to who all lived in very bad sections of Allentown. It didn't matter to me—if I was out partying and needed drugs, I would drive to their homes at 2 or 3 A.M. and knock on their doors to buy drugs. This was before cell phones were common, so even though some of them had pagers, if you wanted something, you had to actually go to the dealer's house. On the nights I was desperate and none of my dealers were holding, I would drive up and down the streets of inner-city Allentown looking to score off anyone who was willing to give me some. I did this more times than I care to recall. A few times I got ripped off when some asshole gave me soap in a baggie instead of crack. But I would actually drive around by myself, roll down my window, and ask total strangers for drugs. Sometimes I had to give them rides to the crack houses to get the drugs. I never had any fear about it and—thankfully and luckily —somehow I managed never to get shot, raped, or killed.

ON SEVERAL OCCASIONS, I HAD BEEN up to State College, Pennsylvania, to party with some high school friends who were going to Penn State. I envied them so much. Their lives seemed so unattainable to me at the time. I could never picture myself going to college or being a student in any way, but a part of me longed for that life. I guess I just felt it was way out of my reach, that I wasn't worthy of school. Many of my friends were talking about moving to Ocean City, Maryland, for the summer, as they did every year. Many college kids went there during the summer for good jobs and to live and party at the beach. I decided that maybe moving there would be a good idea. I was exhausted, sick and tired of living the way I was living.

I was out partying all night every night, getting drunk, doing coke, and smoking crack a lot. I thought maybe a change in scenery would help me. Having just had an abortion, not having a job, and living with my parents were reasons enough for me to want to get away.

I had never really left Pennsylvania on my own before and was excited about the change. I made a couple of calls to friends in State College and made plans to drive to Ocean City with a guy friend I'd known in high school. Suddenly, staying in Allentown for one more minute made me want to crawl out of my skin. My friend was going to pick me up the next day. I went downstairs to my bedroom and started to throw all of my clothes and things into garbage bags. I didn't have any suitcases, since I had never really gone anywhere before. I didn't tell my parents what I was doing. I figured I would call them from Maryland and let them know I wasn't coming back.

I did call my parents on the way. They weren't really upset. They were probably happy to have me out of the house for a while. But they were worried.

My friend showed up early the next day and I threw my two garbage bags full of things in his car and off we went. He asked me where I was going to live, and I just shrugged and said I would figure it out when I got there. I had no idea where I would stay or what I was going to do, but the excitement I felt about leaving was amazing. This was the most spontaneous and adventurous thing I had ever done in my life. Not having a plan as to where I would live or work didn't matter, because as we took to the highway, I felt a freedom that I had never felt before.

I STAYED WITH MY FRIEND at his house in Ocean City for a couple of days and quickly overstayed my welcome. After all, it was a house full of college men, and having some chick camp out on the couch was not their idea of fun.

I called another friend who had a place with several of her sorority sisters and their boyfriends, and I crashed on their couch. We partied every night, drinking and smoking pot. There was no coke around, though. I couldn't believe that none of these college kids did coke, but when I asked about it, they all looked at me like I was a loser, so I never brought it up again. Instead, I went without the coke and just got hammered, usually ending up headfirst puking in the toilet or outside somewhere. I was trying hard to find a job, but since I arrived weeks into the summer season, most of the good jobs were taken already. Things weren't looking good. I was running out of the little money that I had brought with me and I had no food, no place to live, and no job. If that weren't bad enough, I wore out my welcome with the sorority sisters pretty quickly, too, after little more than a week.

I WAS STILL LOOKING FOR A JOB and having a rough time. I went to stay with another person I knew who felt bad that I had come down and had nowhere to stay. So I moved to her place where she was staying with her boyfriend and another couple. They got high all the time, and I loved it.

We all went out one night to this local bar, and I got trashed as usual. I was only nineteen, but I had had a fake Pennsylvania ID for years, and it had always worked to get me into clubs and bars. The first night I went out in Maryland, though, I found a local girl's ID in the bathroom. It was incredible—the girl looked just like me, same eye color and everything. I saw it as a sign that Maryland was where I was meant to be. The best part was that it was a Maryland driver's license, which meant I could get into all the major clubs without paying a cover charge, as was the policy in Ocean City. So I put my Pennsylvania fake ID away and used this random girl's license for the summer. It was great!

I wasn't used to drinking without cocaine to sober me up a bit. So I was drinking like a fish and out of control. Apparently I hit on my friend's boyfriend and threw up in her brand-new car. Needless to say, I wore out my welcome there as well.

THE NEXT DAY I WAS PLANNING TO CALL my parents to come get me. I had spent two weeks freeloading in Ocean City and things were not looking good. I went for a walk, and across the street I saw a sign on a restaurant that said, "Line cook wanted, room and board included." I walked in and was hired on the spot. That night I moved into this great little apartment behind the restaurant with eight other employees. It was a godsend. I got a job and a place to live all in ten minutes. I knew I was supposed to be there.

The people I worked with were all from Maryland and moved there each summer to work for this great little family-owned restaurant. They were good kids who drank but would never think of doing drugs. I decided that I was going to change and not do drugs anymore. However, I ended up drinking every day, all day. This was when I went from primarily partying at night to really becoming an all-day alcoholic. I went to bed with a drink and woke up to a drink. It was normal to drink while you worked there—in fact it was encouraged. While we worked, we drank Miller Lite like it was water. The people I lived with all drank, but not to the extent I did. I remember many nights when I was still up drinking on the porch well into the early hours of the morning while the rest of them were passed out. Or I would stumble to the beach and drink by myself while watching the waves crash onto the sand. I loved the ocean and this was the most time I had ever spent near one. Even through my intoxication, the ocean offered me a peace that was indescribable. I never went on the beach during the day like most of the girls there, who were working hard on their tans. I was there at night, watching the stars and staring into the seemingly endless black abyss. I guess I related to what I saw. It looked how I envisioned my insides looking—like dark, vast, rolling waves crashing inward.

THE SUMMER WAS ONE OF THE BEST I had ever had. I felt as though there might actually be possibilities for me in life. All the people I lived with were in college, and I was starting to think maybe I could go to college, too.

But summer was quickly coming to an end and everyone was gearing up to leave. I began to panic; I didn't want to go home. I looked into some local colleges and thought maybe I could live in Maryland and go to school. For the first time, I thought maybe I could make something of my life—the way the kids I was living with were. Maybe I was worthy of having a good life.

I was out of my mind. After looking over the qualification requirements, I knew I could never get accepted. I had never taken the SAT, and my grade-point average was around 1.5. I knew there was no way I would get in, so I threw away the applications.

I needed to get another job and a new place to live, because the restaurant was closing, which meant the apartment would be emptied out as well. I ended up finding a job at a bar and some locals who needed a roommate. I moved into the place with three other people slightly older than I was and basically freeloaded off them for a couple of months. Two girls and a guy lived there in a place with only two bedrooms, so we were very cramped. They were townies and had access to some drugs—not cocaine like I was used to, but they had pot, and one night we did some acid on the beach. I started hanging out at the only local bars that were open at that time of year, but the town was desolate. I spent the next two months struggling to get by. Hardly anyone was in town, which meant I made no money, so I could barely make rent and live.

ONE NIGHT, I WAS AT A BAR DRINKING by myself when this little blonde caught my eye. She and her friend were playing pool, and this nasty guy was hitting on her big time. It was obvious that she was totally disgusted by the guy and wanted him to leave her alone. This only fueled the guy's attempts more. I watched for a little bit, getting totally annoyed by the guy. I had drunk a couple beers and done two shots, so I was feeling pretty good about myself. I decided to intervene.

I walked over to the girl and threw my arm around her. I looked right in the guy's eyes and said in a very stern voice, "I think you better leave my girlfriend alone. She isn't interested in your type." It was the boldest thing I had ever done in my life, and I was scared shitless. The girl threw her arm around my waist and immediately signed onto my scam, adding, "Yeah, beat it, buddy." The guy looked at us with disgust and walked away muttering, "Fucking dykes." The girl and I looked at each other and burst into laughter. She offered to buy me a beer for my chivalry and I accepted. She was gorgeous and petite, with a great smile and big blue eyes. We hung out together, getting ripped out of our minds for about two hours.

Then her husband showed up. They had just gotten married, and he seemed pretty cool. She told him what had happened. He thought it was hilarious and bought me a shot. I was loaded at this point and riding an incredible high of self-esteem.

I EXCUSED MYSELF TO GO TO THE BATHROOM. When I came out of the stall, the blonde girl was standing at the sink. I walked over to wash my hands. She started rambling on about something and asked if I would wait while she peed. I said, "No problem" and jumped up to sit on the sink. She came out of the stall and smiled at me. She washed her hands, and while she was drying them, she looked at me with these amazing blue eyes and pushed herself between my legs. She put her hands around my waist and continued to look deep into my eyes. My stomach was doing flips and I thought I might be sick, but sick with excitement beyond anything I could ever explain. She held my gaze for a few very intense moments and then slowly she tilted her head and moved in to kiss me. I closed my eyes, and when her lips touched mine, I thought my whole body was going to melt. She had the softest lips I had ever felt in my life, and as her tongue quickly darted into my mouth, I got so excited I couldn't breathe.

As our tongues tangled, my mind was spinning a mile a minute. I couldn't believe this was happening, and I couldn't believe how amazing it felt. I actually felt like there were fireworks going off above our heads, the way they do in cheesy movies. I had never felt so alive in my life. She pulled away from me, and I must have had a dumbass look on my face, because she started laughing uncontrollably and asked if I was okay. I shook my head. I was mesmerized and scared at the same time.

We spent the rest of the night hanging out, and when we got up to leave, she asked if I wanted to come to her place. I was so excited that I agreed. Her husband drove, and during the ride, I got an uncomfortable feeling that they might have had more in mind than what I was okay with. First off, I had never done anything with a woman, and second, I was not about to engage in some type of threesome with a married couple.

When we got to the house, I pulled her aside and said, "Listen, I am not okay with this, and I think I should just go home." She begged me to stay and said I could sleep on the couch. So I did. She pulled out some pillows and a blanket and tucked me into bed. Then she gave me a small kiss and went off to her bedroom with her husband. I felt like a little kid and fell asleep with a smile on my face.

I woke up, opening my eyes to see a little boy staring at me, and I forgot where I was for a second. I jumped up and began to recall the events of the evening. I was feeling very odd, filled with guilt, as I realized that this woman also had a child. I was totally uncomfortable and asked her to drive me home, and she did. She said they were having a tattoo party that night and begged me to come. I really didn't want to, but as soon as she looked at me and those big blue eyes locked with mine, I said yes.

That night I found myself at her party with a bunch of people I had never met before. Two tattoo artists were giving everyone tattoos. I was drinking a lot and starting to feel pretty good when Blue Eyes came over to me and insisted that I let her buy me my first tattoo. At first I totally refused. I told her she was crazy. But she looked at me and said she wanted me to have something to remind me of her and our "moment" together. This was the cheesiest thing I had ever heard, but I also found it quite endearing and could not say no to this woman. I agreed, and she picked out a small red and yellow tie-dyed rose for my ankle. Ten minutes later, this guy was sticking me with a needle as I got my first tattoo.

A COUPLE OF WEEKS LATER, I decided it was time for me to hightail it out of Maryland. I had no money and the town was cold. I never spoke to Blue Eyes, not even to tell her good-bye. I knew she had given me a gift that would both haunt and change me deeply, and it wasn't only the tattoo. Rather, she gave me the realization that my feelings for women had not gone away. The reality of that kiss and the way it rocked my soul to the core was something I was not quite ready to deal with. It had scared the shit out of me. I thought, "Well, maybe I am bisexual," and if so, I would just have to see what that meant. I felt as though I had accomplished some things in Maryland. It had been months since I had done cocaine or crack, and I had a little bit of an understanding of who I was and who I wanted to become.

18

Attempting Recovery

URING THE LONG DRIVE HOME from Maryland
with my parents, I thought maybe my life could
be different, maybe I could start anew, get on a
new path. I could get a job and possibly look into going
to college. We pulled up to our house, and the phone was
already ringing when we walked in. I picked it up and
heard one of my old friends calling to see if I wanted to
go out. I said yes and ended up at the same bar where I
used to hang out all the time. I wound up at someone's
house smoking crack all night. It was literally as though
I had never left. I fell right back in step with the same
people and same shit.

I did end up meeting someone that night who would
help change my life in many ways. His name was Jake,
and he was huge, about six-foot-two or so, with very long
red hair. He was a lead singer in a local band, and we hit it
off right away, with one exception: Jake didn't do drugs or
look kindly upon those who did.

We began spending every day together and really
developed an amazing connection; he was one of my
soul mates. I don't believe in having only one soul mate.
It doesn't even remotely make sense to me that you

stumble around the world searching for that one person to complete you. I think we have many soul mates, and if we are lucky, we can find several of them along this journey.

Jake really understood me and was totally in sync with who I was. He knew about my attraction to women, and he encouraged it. He had a very strong feminine side, and he was man enough to express it. We would go to gay bars, and he would tell me to go and be myself, and I would. I would find a girl and start dancing with her and eventually make out with her, and Jake would watch. He never tried to get involved. He didn't pressure me about bringing someone home—although he wouldn't have objected if I had. It wasn't for lack of trying. I would hook up with a girl, and when it came time to go home, she would want me to come home with her—until I told her I had a boyfriend. Then she would get pissed off and basically tell me where to go. I found out quickly that *real* lesbians don't share that heterosexual fantasy of going home with a straight couple.

I think Jake truly knew it was in my heart and a larger part of me than I ever knew at the time, and he embraced it. He used to joke with me that if we broke up I would wind up gay. I always laughed it off.

I actually enjoyed sex with Jake. He was really the first man I could say that about. There was still a moment or two during sex when I didn't feel right, but overall I felt very safe and secure with him. That was a new feeling for me. I had never known anyone who took enough time to care about me on the level that he did. I really wanted the relationship to work. My dad and stepmother really liked Jake, too, and I know they hoped my life would straighten out because I was with him.

I EVEN INTRODUCED HIM TO MY MOTHER ONCE, which was a disaster. We went to visit her at a car show she and her current boyfriend were attending. I had recently turned twenty-one. For my birthday, I had gotten my tongue pierced and added a long vine and another rose to the tattoo the blonde had given me in Maryland. When I saw my mom and introduced her to Jake, she didn't notice the tongue ring right away. We talked with her for a little bit, and when she did notice it she just laughed and asked me, "What did you do that for?" I casually replied that I'd done it because I wanted to and that it was fun to have. Then my mother looked at me and said, "Well aren't they also supposed to enhance blow jobs?" I just stared at her. An embarrassed smile came across my face, and Jake just looked at me. She then looked Jake right in the eye and said in a very flirty way, "Isn't it sad my daughter has to get something like that to give good head?" Then she laughed and turned on her heel to walk over to her boyfriend.

Jake's jaw dropped as he looked at me. I nodded my head, mortified, and just said, "Yep, that's my mom."

I TRIED HARD TO BE GOOD and not go out and get high, but my patterns of drinking and doing lots of cocaine were so ingrained in me that it just never seemed to work out that way. I could no longer drink without craving cocaine and needing it. I would get to a point in drinking at which I would teeter on the edge of intoxication, and then something in me would click, and I would be on a mission to find cocaine. Mainly, I wanted the coke so I could stay out and drink more.

Jake and I fought back and forth about this cycle for months, and finally one night, he'd had enough and dumped me. It crushed me. I was very much in love with him and had never felt heartache like that before. I truly felt like my heart was ripped out of my chest.

I remember sitting on my bed after getting off the phone with him and sobbing so loudly I could barely breathe. My father came down to my room and asked what was wrong. I told him about Jake. For the first time in my life, my father held me as I cried. He normally avoided any expression of emotion with the exception of anger. I will never forget the way it felt to have him hold me while I cried. If only I had had that years ago at the times when I most needed it.

I DECIDED THAT I WAS GOING TO CHANGE MY WAYS and try to win Jake back. I had begun having memories and flashbacks of the night I was sexually assaulted when I was twelve. I believed this was the root of my problems, where all my issues stemmed from. I had a desire to begin revisiting that night. I was working at a chiropractor's office as an assistant, and one of the patients there was a counselor. She was also gay, which very much intrigued me. I decided to start seeing her professionally. The sessions were good; I was as honest as I could be at that time, which was rather limited but definitely more open than I had ever been in my life. We talked about Jake, my use of drugs and alcohol, my sexuality, and the assault. It was in those sessions that I first began to realize that I might have a problem.

She talked to me about Alcoholics Anonymous (AA), and I was totally freaked out. I thought that those people were old drunks who went to sit and chant in some cult-like environment. I was skeptical, to say the least, but nonetheless decided to try it. I was desperate to change and win Jake back, even though during these sessions I was seriously attracted to my therapist. I was still not ready to fully accept my sexuality, and I did really love Jake. I decided to go to an AA meeting. I called the AA hotline and the person on the other end informed me where the meetings were and asked if I needed a ride. I wrote down the address, politely thanked the person, and said I had a vehicle.

AS I PULLED UP TO THE ADDRESS, I noticed it was a church. I got nervous. I did not like churches and always felt very uncomfortable in them. Several people were milling about the front door, smoking and drinking coffee. I walked up and finished the cigarette I was smoking. I took one last very deep puff and held it in for dear life. I exhaled, stubbed it out in the ashtray, and walked into the church. There were lots of chairs all lined up in nice rows and a table in the front with a microphone and people sitting. I was very uncomfortable, my hands were cold and clammy, and I kept my head down the whole time. I quickly took a seat in the very back of the room and listened as some guy began reading a bunch of shit that made no real sense to me. I wasn't hearing anything he was saying. I felt sick and was struck by how many people were in the room. I was the youngest person there. Just as I had suspected, it was an old drunks' club. One guy kept looking at me; every time he did my skin crawled. He gave me the creeps. I wanted to get up and leave a million times but I held in there as several people raised their hands for the main guy to call upon them to speak.

I listened to people talk about how hard it was to stay sober and heard a whole bunch of weird slogans, like "Keep it simple" and "One day at a time." After someone spoke, people kept saying, "Thanks for sharing. Keep coming back." It was weird, and I wanted out.

The meeting finally came to end; the hour had seemed like an eternity, and I had already made up my mind that this was not the place for me. I was not an alcoholic. At the end of the meeting, everyone got up and began to form a circle. I had no clue what the hell was going on until someone grabbed my hand and said, "We have to close the meeting." I was freaking clueless and totally uncomfortable as I stood holding two complete strangers' hands. Someone said a few words and then all at once everyone began chanting, "God, grant me the serenity to accept the things I cannot change, the courage to change the things I can, and the wisdom to know the difference." They finished by saying, "Keep coming back. It works if you work it." I thought they were all fucking nuts, and I wanted nothing more than to run for the door.

I began walking toward the door and the guy who had been staring at me approached. He asked if this was my first time, and I replied yes. He then proceeded to tell me about some dance somewhere and asked if I wanted to go with him. I was disgusted that this slime bucket would have the nerve to hit on me at an AA meeting. And it was all I needed, a nice excuse in my mind for not going back. I told my counselor the next day what had transpired and that AA could not help me. I was not one of "them" and was not willing to go back. I could tell she was disappointed but she seemed to understand. She asked if I would be willing to go to a group for kids more my age. I agreed.

AT THIS POINT I HAD NOT HAD A DRINK in like ten days, which was a record for me. I was spending a lot of time at home with my parents and in my room working out and meditating—two things I had never done before. I was feeling good, actually better than I had ever felt before. I did, however, still smoke pot. In fact, when I decided to quit drinking, I took up pot pretty heavily. I figured that pot was not bad, that I had never had a blackout while smoking dope, never got in trouble while smoking dope. All that ever happened was that I laughed a lot and got hungry. Besides, it made the meditation all that much more real. I felt connected. I began dressing a little more hippie-like, putting my hair in dreadlocks and wearing long skirts. I liked my new look. I felt free and spiritual.

My therapist gave me the address to the teen group she wanted me to attend. When I arrived I was greeted by a counselor who gave me a ton of paperwork to fill out, asking me every question you can imagine about three times, including name, Social Security number, date of birth, etc. This was a standard intake and assessment of my so-called alcohol problem. I had to take a test that had several questions about my drinking patterns. I answered yes to them all, which I felt pretty good about, until the counselor there told me that, if I answered yes to one or more questions, I was probably an alcoholic. She told me about a group of young people that met once a week, a support group for young alcoholics and addicts. I informed her that I was pretty sure I wasn't an alcoholic and that I just had some issues I needed to deal with. She quietly smiled a little smile, handed me the paper with the information on it and said, "See you in group."

I DECIDED TO GO THE NEXT NIGHT, even though I was pretty sure I wasn't an alcoholic. I wanted Jake back more than anything. And my parents were so pleased with my sudden change in behavior, that I thought maybe I would give it a try. I thought that if I went, I could show them I was getting help and doing well.

I pulled up at the address the counselor gave me and saw a similar scene outside the building—a bunch of people smoking and drinking coffee—but this time they were all young. I was relieved to see people my age, but I still felt pretty sure I didn't belong there. The same counselor who had done my intake and told me about the group greeted us, and I followed everyone into a little room with sofas and chairs. The counselor began the session with ground rules, and then people began going around the room and introducing themselves. Each person said his or her first name and then followed it by saying, "I'm an addict" or "I'm an alcoholic" or both. When it came to my turn, I simply said, "My name is Jennifer, and I have no idea why I am here." They all looked at me, some with amused looks on their faces and a couple with anger and hatred. I listened to them, and while they spoke of being alcoholics and addicts, I rationalized every word they said in my own head to refute any feeling of association I may have been feeling. I might have been willing to stop drinking for a while, but this was ridiculous. I wasn't going to sit in a room and dump my feelings out like a wimp. I sat with my hands crossed tightly over my chest and looked at my feet the whole time. My stubborn side kicked in big time, and I was not open to anything anyone was saying. All I heard was noise.

I went a couple of times mainly because I was trying to be good, trying to do what I thought would make my parents happy and win Jake back. After each time, I headed over to one of my local hang-out bars to meet up with my friends. I wouldn't drink, but I would immediately get stoned. It felt good and almost empowering to walk into a bar and not drink. I enjoyed it. I figured I had the whole issue licked: I didn't have to drink, I could just hang out and get high and go home at a decent hour. After a month of not drinking and of going to the group and then the bar, I was feeling pretty good about myself. My parents were very proud of me because even though I had been laid off from the chiropractor's office, I was coming home at decent hours and getting up and functioning.

ONE NIGHT AFTER GROUP, I went to the bar to hang out and was feeling particularly good about myself. A friend was ordering Jägermeister shots as I walked in. As I sat down next to him, he pushed a shot in front of me and asked, "You in?" I looked at him and thought, "What the hell? I have been so good lately." I slammed the shot back fast and felt the rip of heat burn down the back of my throat. It warmed my stomach and I felt home again. About three hours and many more shots and drinks later, I found myself at a friend's house smoking crack. So much for changing my ways. I was right back where I had left off a little over a month ago—and all it had taken was one shot.

19
Losing My Mother

MY MOTHER BEGAN GETTING SICK AGAIN. Her breast cancer had come back, and this time, it was spreading to her lymph nodes. The doctors had suggested chemotherapy as a treatment, which would mean she would lose her hair and be very sick. She had a shunt implanted into her chest so that they could just plug her into the machine to give her treatments. I remember her showing it to me one day and I just shuddered. I could barely look at it. I didn't want to see her that way. So instead, I avoided seeing her at all. I would call but I couldn't bring myself to visit often.

There was also no hope in sight for Jake and me to reconcile, which made me very depressed. My brother Brian had just begun singing for a pretty good band, and I began dating the bass-guitar player, who was a huge partier. Several of the other band members smoked a lot of crack, and although my boyfriend partied, he didn't smoke crack. I found myself turning to this drug once again after my mom got sick. I was out every night drinking more than I ever had and doing coke and smoking crack like it was my job. I just kept going out every night, getting deeper into using, which meant I was missing a lot of work at the travel agency where I'd been hired.

MY FATHER ALWAYS MARVELED at how good I was at getting amazing jobs with few to no qualifications. I had a knack for always finding really good jobs and getting hired. It was just keeping them that always caused me a slight problem. After being laid off at the chiropractor's office, I came upon a newspaper ad for a travel agency that was looking for new recruits. I thought, "What the hell— I would like to travel. Why not?" I submitted my résumé and got an interview within a week. I landed the job on the spot and started training right away. I fell in love with the job; it was a great corporation with excellent benefits and a decent salary. The job also had many great perks, like free airplane tickets and hotel vouchers. I learned everything quickly, as always, and was excelling at the job.

But with my mother's cancer back and my loss of Jake permanent, I was so caught up in partying and trying to not care that I ended up losing the job at the travel agency. I called in for days off far too often. My boss couldn't make excuses for me anymore, nor could she accept mine. It crushed me the day I lost that job, because it was such an amazing position, but I walked out of the office and went out to get high to forget about it.

I looked for another job in travel and found one within a couple of weeks. This job required me to attend training in Atlanta. I was totally excited, because I loved to travel but had only flown once before. I spoke to my mother right before I left. She didn't sound good at all. She was getting heavy chemo at this time and was simply giving up on life. I couldn't bring myself to visit her much, because it was far too painful to see her with no hair and dying. It was easier to get drunk and high and forget. I still called her daily, as I had done all my life, and she still had enough strength to give me shit on a daily basis. Some things never change.

WHEN I CAME HOME FROM THE TRIP, I received a phone call from my mother. She said she wasn't feeling well and that her back was killing her. She ended up going to the hospital because it was so painful. I met her and my brothers at St. Luke's Hospital in Easton. She was hooked up to an IV and a couple of machines, and she looked terrible. She was in a lot of pain. I went to her side and gave her a hug and kiss as the doctor walked in to give me and my brothers the scoop on what was going on. He said her cancer was progressing, and it didn't look as though she would be able to live alone anymore without help. He suggested that we look into a nursing home for her. Both my brothers were furious; they didn't want anything to do with her going anywhere. The three of us argued over what to do. I said I would handle everything. My oldest brother, Jimmy, shot me a look of death and said, "Oh, so now you want to do something for her, when you're never even around." The guilt he'd flung hit my face like ice, but I met his stare and said, "Yes." Neither of my brothers wanted anything to do with it.

I spoke with the doctor and decided to start calling places to see where she could go and what we could do. I spoke with my mother briefly and found out that she had not made any plans in the event of her death. Basically, she had been in denial about the fact that she was dying or had simply given up and didn't care. Either way, the woman had nothing. No will. No plans. Nothing. I went home that night and talked with my dad about what we should do. We began calling nursing homes to see where we could put her and to make the necessary arrangements.

I WENT BACK TO THE HOSPITAL THAT NIGHT and sat with my mother. It was actually the first time she and I spent several hours together without fighting. She was in a tremendous amount of pain and had a morphine drip next to her bed. She couldn't eat or drink anything. She was very thirsty and her lips were cracking. I got some ice chips from the nurse and sat on the side of the bed as I traced her sore lips slowly with the ice chips. Her face was so pale and she looked so frail. She only had a very small amount of hair left on her head, and most of her eyebrows were gone. We sat together for a long time. We didn't really say much, just looked into each other's eyes and silently loved one another. I rubbed her head and continued to feed her the ice chips. It was the most loving gesture I could have done for her, and I can't really explain it, but as we sat there in silence looking at each other, it was like all the past shit from our long and tormented relationship started to go away. We were making amends with one another just by looking at each other. She made a couple of jokes and we laughed a lot. It was a wonderful night—probably one of the best my mother and I had ever had together. I left late that night. My brothers had come and gone. They were not handling things well at all.

I DECIDED NOT TO GO OUT AFTER THE HOSPITAL and went home instead. I talked with Dad and Pat for a little while and then went to bed. I was exhausted and for some reason had no desire to get high or drunk. I called off work the next day so I could spend more time with my mother. When I arrived at the hospital the next day,

I walked into my mom's room and she was sleeping. My brothers came soon after, and we sat around making idle chitchat. The doctor came in and asked to speak with us in the family waiting room. I told him that I had begun to look into nursing homes, but he cut me off in midsentence. He said, "Your mother is very sick, and it doesn't appear that she will be making it out of the hospital. You need to prepare yourselves for her death, which is imminent." My heart dropped to my feet. I looked at him, and both my brothers freaked out. He said it was only a matter of time, that she was getting worse by the hour. He said that because she didn't have a living will or anything, someone would need to be responsible for her. My brothers and I argued for a moment as to who was going to take care of everything, and it became abundantly clear that the responsibility was going to fall to me, which was fine. I felt a sense of strength that I didn't remember having before.

I left the hospital and met with my father to begin discussing all the things that needed to be done. I had to get a lawyer and have a document granting me power of attorney drawn up and signed quickly. I stood by my mother's bedside with the document shaking in my hand. The power of attorney basically gave me all legal rights over my mother, and the thought of that seemed so strange to me. That she was so sick she couldn't make her own decisions felt so wrong to me. But each day she had been growing weaker, and on this day she could barely keep her eyes open. I needed her to sign the paper. I explained to her what it was for, that I would be handling all her arrangements and medical concerns. She nodded in acknowledgment and attempted to sign. She was barely able to write a squiggly line before she dropped the pen.

My mother's signature was something I had always admired for some reason. She had big, circular, beautiful lettering when she wrote, and it was very distinctive. I used to trace her name until I had her signature down pat for the million times in the past that I had forged it for school paperwork. I guess because I have her hands it was easy for me to emulate her writing. If I try, even today my handwriting can look just like hers. That day, though, I took the paper with her squiggle and kissed her forehead.

I HAD A TON OF WORK TO DO, and she was not looking good. I had to arrange a funeral, handle her accounts, deal with her insurance, decide what to do with her belongings. Since she had no will, and she was beyond the ability to speak freely about her wishes, I had to make each and every decision. I began with her insurance; I went to her job and informed them what was happening. I went to a funeral home in town the next day with my father.

Her life-insurance policy stated that the three children and her mother would be her beneficiaries. I changed the policy to pay out the expenses of the funeral first and then the benefits to the rest to us. I knew if I left it up to everyone to collectively pay for the funeral, it would end up being my expense. So I made the funeral home the first beneficiary. Then I closed her checking and savings accounts and divided the money among me, my brothers, and my grandmother.

MY FATHER WAS STOIC THROUGH EVERYTHING; he gave me rides wherever I needed to go and lent his silent support throughout the work I had to do. My brothers were off doing their own things and were not willing or able to help me. I had no desire to drink or get high during this process. I don't know why, seeing as it had been such a daily coping mechanism for me. I was on autopilot in a way, mechanically going through a million motions at once without feeling a thing, but also without any chemical or alcohol assistance.

Being at the funeral home was the eeriest thing I had ever had to do. Here I was, planning a funeral for a person who was still alive. I sat with the funeral director and planned how everything would go on the day of the funeral. We picked out thank-you cards and a sign-in book and wrote her obituary. That was the hardest part. I had to write my mother's obituary, and I hadn't a clue how to do it. The funeral director was so kind to me, asking me questions while he filled in the blanks on a standard obituary: She is survived by her two sons and daughter, and such and such. It was surreal.

The next step was the worst part. Brian finally showed up to help me pick out the casket. We walked around a room filled with caskets, not totally grasping the idea that our mother would be lying in one shortly. We settled on a beautiful blue one and left. Brian was a mess and didn't speak much. I just kept on working. It is so weird, but if you don't plan for this stuff, you don't realize how much needs to be done when someone dies.

My next item was to find a burial place. I struggled for a while with an appropriate cemetery. I didn't know where she wanted to be buried, and I didn't want to make a bad mistake.

That night, I went to the hospital and sat with my mom and talked to her. At this time, she was slowly slipping into a morphine coma. The doctor said she was in a lot of pain and it was up to me to approve increasing the dosage of morphine. I didn't want her to be in pain, but

I also didn't want her going into a coma. I was scared but made the decision to increase her dosage so she would be comfortable. She gently slipped into a coma and the room felt very quiet. Just the low sounds of the machines that were keeping her alive.

I sat and talked with her, asking where she would like to be buried. I knew she couldn't answer me, but I kept talking. Somehow a memory of my childhood came rushing back to me. When we lived in Nazareth, which to my recollection was the happiest our family had been, my brothers used to play baseball. I went to each game, and adjacent to the baseball field was a cemetery where I would play. I decided to look into that cemetery, as it seemed to be the most appropriate place.

My father seemed to agree. The next day I called and inquired about burial plots. I spoke with a guy on the phone and explained my situation. He mentioned that it was a good idea to buy several in a row so that our whole family could be next to each other. It made sense, so I bought five plots: one for my mother, two for my brothers, one for my grandmother, and one for myself, even though I was pretty sure I would never want to actually be buried. Never in a million years would I have thought that I would be buying burial plots for myself and my family. It was such an odd feeling.

AFTERWARD, HAVING COMPLETED ALMOST ALL my tasks, I headed toward the hospital. By this time, word had spread to my mother's overly dramatic, drug- and alcohol-ridden family, and her room was packed with aunts, uncles, and cousins I hadn't seen in years. When I got there, as usual, everyone was feeling so sorry for themselves in the incredibly selfish way that addicts can.

Some were crying and saying, "How can this be happening to me? I can't believe my sister is dying." I wondered why it mattered since they didn't bother with her in life. But again, that is a side effect of addiction; everything is all about the addict. The display made me sick to my stomach, and my father was not in the mood to deal with it. He politely said hello to everyone and then informed me that he was going home and I could call him when I needed a ride.

My mother was not doing well at all. She looked very pale and swollen. When I sat down next to her and touched her arm, it was cold, and as I squeezed her hand, my fingers sank into her skin and left an impression as though it were Play-Doh. I freaked out. She felt as though she were filled with a ton of fluid. I asked the doctor to come in. When he arrived, he informed us that it would be only a matter of hours before my mother died, that she had a very strong heart but the rest of her body was slowly giving out.

The various family members in the room broke out in cries and screams. The doctor said it would be a good time for everyone to say their good-byes. So one by one, everyone took turns sitting with my mother and saying good-bye. I wondered what half of them were saying: "Gee, sorry I haven't seen you in like ten years, but I love you so much." I was angry that I had to share the time with them, but I kept that reaction to myself. The room was dark and dreary. The blinds were pulled, and after everyone said their good-byes, we all sat around waiting.

HAVE YOU EVER WAITED FOR SOMEONE TO DIE? It is the slowest, most agonizing thing in the world. We held on to every breath she took, each of us wondering if it would be the last. We sat for hours like this, although it seemed like time stood still. At times, I sat and held her and prayed for her to pass so she could be released from the pain. I knew she must have been so annoyed at all the family arriving and being so dramatic around her. I could feel inside that she was not at peace. I wanted everyone to leave but didn't have the heart to actually say it. Slowly, as the hours passed, people began to leave. After all, it was getting late and there was drinking to be done. My brothers decided to go out with my aunt to get beer and drink in the parking lot, which I thought was a rather disgusting idea, but I didn't say anything.

My two younger cousins and I were left in the room. I was so pleased to have everyone gone, and I was exhausted with the gloomy environment. I looked at my cousins and told them I couldn't take this dreary room anymore. I turned on the light and switched on the TV that was hanging in the corner. They both seemed as relieved as I was. We had been sitting in the dark for hours just waiting, and it was too much. As I sat at the side of the bed watching TV, I heard a tiny noise come from my mother's mouth. Looking over at her, I saw that she was attempting to say something and that her eyes were fluttering. I quickly turned the TV off, rushed to her, got into bed with her, and held her. I forgot my cousins' presence as I focused on her.

She opened her eyes and looked right at me as if she had been waking from sleep. Her eyes focused on mine, and she began to mutter something that I couldn't make out. I held her and continued to look in her eyes. As I caressed her bald head, I told her that I loved her and that it was okay to let go now. I told her to go to the angels that were waiting for her. I kept repeating "I love you, Mom" and "It's okay to go" over and over again. I watched as she struggled for air, and slowly the life left her big brown eyes. I watched as God took my mother from her body, and I held her. It was the most beautiful moment I had ever had in my life. I held her as the life slipped from her body, and I surrounded her with all the love I had in me.

Her head fell to my side and a brownish-green bile-like substance spilled from her mouth. Cancer, I thought; that is what cancer physically looks like. It was sickness flowing from her mouth, and I knew that was the horrible, evil substance that had ravaged her body. I could picture her insides being attacked and slowly eaten by the nasty slime. I shuddered, grabbed a tissue, and quickly wiped it away.

Then I just held her tighter, tears flowing out of my eyes like a faucet, and I cried as I rocked back and forth with my now-dead mother in my arms. I cried and cried until a low howl crawled up my throat and out of my mouth. I screamed as my brothers rushed into the room with my mother's boyfriend, who had just arrived to see her. My brothers began to sob next to her.

I stopped screaming, stopped crying, and gently released my mother as I got out of the bed. The autopilot mode that I had been in all week quickly returned, and I went out to get the nurse. I told her that I needed my mother's things. She gave me the belongings that my mother had brought with her when she had come into the hospital. After my brothers said their good-byes, I called my father and told him. I then called everyone else: my grandmother, my aunts, and anyone else who had left word that they wanted to know when she passed. My brothers and I left the hospital, and I went with Jimmy to his apartment. I didn't want him to be alone that night. The whole night I had this amazing feeling that I still to this day cannot explain. It was like a warm blanket surrounded me.

I felt protected and encased by love. I knew in my heart it was my mother's spirit surrounding me. She had yet to leave me. I felt her, and it was so comforting and calming.

BEING WITH HER AND HOLDING HER while she died was the most amazing experience I have ever had. It was heartbreaking, yes, but it was also magical. The woman who brought me into this world, the woman with whom I had a tumultuous relationship for so many years, was now surrounding me with all the love she could never give me in life. She was giving it to me in death, and I will never forget that feeling for as long as I live. It was as if we could never have made amends for all the wrongs we had done to each other in life, so instead we made amends nonverbally through our eyes as they locked with one another before she died. I believed in my heart that my mother was waiting for me to be alone in the room with her just for that purpose, so we could share that moment. So she could die in peace and I could live in peace. She brought me into this world, and I had the awesome responsibility of seeing her out of it. It was amazing. I held on to that feeling all night long. In the morning when I woke up, it was gone, and I felt cold and alone. I knew she was gone.

I WALKED IN THROUGH THE FRONT DOOR of the funeral home with my brothers and my father. We arrived early for the family viewing, before all the other people came to pay their last respects. I hadn't seen my mom since I had left the hospital. I had a terrible feeling in my stomach about seeing her in the casket that I had purchased just days before. I had been to so many funerals and seen so many bodies lying in caskets, and they never looked the way I remembered them. I have never seen one dead person actually look good. I often think open-casket viewings are morbid. I understand the concept behind people needing to see the person for validation. But it is still creepy and leaves an image in my mind that I am not certain anyone should ever really have. We have such odd customs in our society. We gather around the dead and mourn the loss we feel in ourselves; we do not really mourn the person. I think it is a rather selfish and dramatic ritual, but then again, that makes sense in America. We are a selfish and odd culture.

We slowly entered the room where my mother lay lifeless in the blue casket. As soon as I saw her, my stomach fell and my breath left my throat. I could not breathe. I began to sob hysterically. I couldn't control it as I looked at her pale face. Her lips were sewn together and her eyes were closed. She wore one of her brown wigs that never quite looked like her own hair. She had her blue star-sapphire ring on her hand. I had never seen my mother's hand without it. She wore her gold necklace and her high school class ring. I finally composed myself enough to get close to the side of the casket. I felt sick and panicky—it didn't feel real. What had happened to that peaceful feeling I had when she died?

I slowly lifted my hand to her face to caress her cheek and grazed her cheekbone with my warm finger. Her face felt cold and stiff. I was immediately freaked out and flinched, pulling my hand back. I struggled through the viewing while my closest friends and family gathered to say good-bye and droves of people poured in, some I hadn't seen in years, some I had never met before. It felt so odd to be greeted by so many people. I gave and received more hugs that day than I had in my whole life.

We finally left the funeral and went to a bar, where I proceeded to get drunk—drunker than I had been in a long time. It was time to drown the pain, and I did. I don't remember that night or the three months that followed very well, because I was drowning.

20

Living High, Hitting a Low

THE NEXT THREE MONTHS WERE A BLUR. I lost my job at the second travel agency, too, because the managers said I took too much time off for my mother's death. I promptly told them to go fuck themselves. Who were they to determine my bereavement?

I didn't care.

I didn't care about anything.

I felt so empty inside that if you had cut my chest open there would have been an empty black hole staring back at you, with tiny demons floating around, lost and screaming silently in pain. But they couldn't get out. I couldn't even think of how to begin to heal from this pain; it was so much bigger than me, bigger than any other pain I had endured. I had no way of knowing how to even begin to grieve the loss of my mother, because I had never really grieved anything in my life.

The pain was too much to bear, and it started to take over my mind, body, and spirit.

I quickly got a job at a college-oriented bar in Bethlehem that seemed rather convenient to me, because I could drink as much as I wanted there and make money at the same time. Worked for me. I made some good connections there.

The manager and the head cook were crack addicts; they quickly became my new best friends. I usually worked 4 P.M. to closing. We would start our days with a couple of shots while working. It was customary to drink with the customers, which was great for me, since I was trying to ensure that I was intoxicated at all times. I couldn't deal with the empty pit, so I filled it daily with booze and drugs.

Usually by around 7 P.M. or so, just when I had enough tip money in my pocket, the manager, the chef, and I would place our nightly crack order. Our dealer was a regular at the bar and made a nightly run for us. When the crack arrived, we would go downstairs to the basement, into the dry storage room where we kept our pipe and lighter. We would each go down individually, do a hit of crack, and then set up for the next person, so we weren't all down there at the same time.

It was a great escape for me. I was constantly numb, which was how I wanted to be.

I HAD A SETTLEMENT from my mother's estate for $10,000. I was smart enough to give it all to Dad and Pat to hold and monitor so I wouldn't drop it all. They would give me money when I needed it, for example, for furniture and rent when I finally moved out, but only in small portions. Otherwise, I would have smoked it all up in a weekend if I had had full access to it.

I was still living with my parents at this time. I began staying out all night long and not coming in until the wee hours of the morning. My parents would look at me with shame and powerlessness. It was painful to see in their eyes that look of disapproval and the pain they felt. They knew I was unreachable and so did I, but we would make small talk and try to pretend that things were normal.

My brother Jimmy's girlfriend Heather was pregnant at the time, and everyone was excited about the idea of a baby in the family. I guess the thought of life coming into our family was refreshing, and it was the first grandchild. Jimmy was destroyed by the fact that our mother would never meet his little girl. I went over to his apartment often and helped them prepare the room for her. I was close to his girlfriend, since we had partied heavily together before she got pregnant. She asked me to be in the room when the baby was born, and I felt honored.

The night before the baby was born, I was working at the bar. That night we stayed late after the bar closed and partied until about 9 A.M. The manager finally drove me home.

I felt like shit. I was so drunk and coming down from smoking crack all night. I could barely hold my head up, and my body ached so badly. As I crawled into the house, I passed my parents, who just looked at me with disgust.

They briefly mentioned that my brother had called to say his girlfriend had gone into labor. My brother would call when the baby was on the way. I went downstairs and said nothing as I crawled into bed. All I cared about was having my head hit the pillow. I drifted off to sleep, until the phone rang next to my head and woke me. I stumbled over to the receiver, put it to my ear, and heard my brother's voice filled with excitement. "Jen, the baby is coming. Please tell Dad and Pat."

I mumbled something, hung up, and promptly fell right back to sleep. I woke up hours later only to realize that I had missed the entire birth of my first niece. My family was furious with me, and I was so ashamed of myself. Not only did I miss it, but my parents almost did as well, because I never told them my brother called. That day

Cheyanne Alexis Mara Storm was born, and I missed the whole thing.

I was so filled with guilt that I didn't go to see her for a couple of weeks. My parents were simply disgusted with my actions and me. I knew I had outstayed my welcome and that I needed to move out.

I GOT AN APARTMENT ABOVE THE BAR where I worked. It was very convenient and probably one of the lowest points of my life. The crappy little two-bedroom apartment was surrounded by other addicts and alcoholics like me. Carrie, my friend from high school, moved in with me. She was a cokehead and just as hard a partier as I was, but she always managed to get up and go to work. My parents had given me enough money from my mother's estate to furnish the apartment and pay for the rent for a couple of months. So it was a great deal for her, because she didn't have to pay for anything, but she was never there anyway. She was either working or at her boyfriend's house.

I had also recently purchased a kitten and named her Simba. She was an adorable calico cat who would run all around my little apartment and cuddle up around my neck when I slept. It was nice to have company I didn't have to answer to and who wouldn't judge me.

I had sunk very low, and oddly enough, felt very comfortable at the level I had reached. I was drinking and doing drugs every minute I was awake. I couldn't get enough into my system fast enough. I was in so much pain and using the drink and drugs to cover it up, but things were starting to come to a head. Every now and then, I would catch a glimpse of myself in the mirror, and the image I saw staring back at me was foreign. I was very skinny because I never ate; I would eat once a day, usually at the bar.

On my days off I would sit in my apartment and get drunk by myself. I was so isolated from everyone at this point—other than Carrie on the rare occasion she was home. I stopped calling my family and friends. All I did was work at the bar and get high. It got to the point where I didn't want to venture out into public because I knew people would look into my eyes and see how dead I was inside. They would see the girl with no soul and become intimidated, so I felt it best to stay around those who were like me in the dark corners of the bar and the hallways of my apartment building.

Sometimes I ordered Chinese food from the place across the street. I would say, "Delivery," and then place my order, an egg roll and veggie lo mein. They would ask me my address, and I would tell them. Then they would ask, "Delivery?" And I answered, "Yes, delivery." I didn't even want to walk across the street to pick up food.

I WAS IN HIDING AND PICKLING AWAY in my self-loathing and pain. That was what my life had become. I would get moments of clarity when I knew I didn't want to live the way I was living, but I was so trapped by my addictions that I couldn't move. I vividly remember being at work, placing my nightly crack order, and even though I had handed my money over, not wanting to get high. I would think to myself, "Jennifer, don't do it tonight. You know what happens when you do, and you can never get enough."

It was like someone or something else had control over my actions, because as much as my head would scream "No!" inside, nothing would come out of my mouth. I would stand at the top of the stairs to the basement where the drugs were and just stare at the steps.

Inside my head I was screaming, "No, don't do it. Not this time. Walk away!" But I was guided by something much more powerful, and my feet carried me down the stairs into the dark, dry storage room, where I filled my lungs with the toxic smoke that made all my pain go away.

The kicker was that nothing seemed to be working anymore. It didn't matter how many drinks I had or how many drugs I did; the pain was beginning to overpower the numbness of the drugs. It took more and more alcohol and more and more drugs to numb me, until one night I couldn't get enough and the world came crashing down around me.

ONE DAY I WOKE UP EARLY, because there was a big college football game that day and our bar was tailgating. I started drinking Bloody Marys at 9 A.M., followed by beer around 11 A.M. I was loaded by noon and proceeded to drink all afternoon at the tailgate party.

We all stumbled back to the bar around 3:30 P.M. I landed on a barstool and held court there for several hours, sipping martinis and doing shots with the regulars. I was smashed. I hadn't done any cocaine yet that day, so my chemical balance was off and I got drunker than usual.

At some point, I stumbled into the kitchen looking for a friend. I stumbled toward the stairs and teetered on the top step, swaying back and forth as the room spun around me. My vision was blurred, and the last thing I remember was falling forward. Fortunately, my friend was coming up the stairs at that very moment and caught me before I tumbled down twenty-five steps onto the basement floor.

He carried me into the boiler room and placed me on a cot that some staff members used for power naps. I woke up several hours later still very intoxicated. For a moment,

I didn't know where I was, and then I couldn't remember how I got there. I glanced at my watch to see it was 7 P.M., and I quickly remembered I had a party to go to. It was a thirtieth birthday party for the husband of my best friend from high school. I didn't usually leave the bar, but I had told my friend and her husband that I would be there and didn't want to let anyone down.

I crawled up the stairs and into the bar, which was still packed with college students and locals celebrating the win. I ordered another martini to refresh my buzz and sucked it down quickly. I left the bar and got into my car to drive myself to the party, which I was already late for. I started to drive toward the highway.

I HAD NO BUSINESS BEING BEHIND THE WHEEL, but that didn't faze me, as I had driven drunk more times than I care to recall. I never got a DUI ticket or was in an accident with another vehicle while drunk, but I did occasionally bounce off curbs and poles and somehow always managed to smash my taillights.

I often came out to find my father duct-taping my lights onto my car. I would always make some excuse, like someone at the mall must have hit me or I had accidentally hit something. The truth was that I never remembered what I hit or what I did.

WHEN I WAS ABOUT NINETEEN and living with Doug, I took out a $1,200 loan to purchase a gold Chevy Cavalier, which amazed me because it was my first time getting credit for anything. Shortly after I moved back in with my parents, I was doing temp work at an insurance company in Bethlehem. On one random weekday night, I stayed out till 4 A.M. getting hammered as usual and then came home to crash for an hour and get up for work. I didn't really get any sleep; it was more like a momentary rest for my body. So I was a mess that day while driving on Route 22, where traffic was bad and often just stopped abruptly.

That morning during rush hour, I do not remember exactly how it happened, except that one minute I was driving, and the next moment, traffic was at a standstill. I slammed on my brakes as hard as I could. I stopped just in time before hitting the car in front of me and momentarily thought I was fine, but suddenly I was pushed hard from behind by another vehicle. The thrust of the hit pushed my car forward. For whatever reason, I instinctively threw my body onto the passenger side and covered my head quickly with my hands. After all was said and done, ten cars crashed and piled up.

When I finally lifted myself up to see the wreckage, my whole body was shaking. I saw car parts scattered all over the highway. Somehow I was now directly behind the vehicle that had struck me from behind. I still don't know exactly how he hit me from behind with me ending up behind him.

My car was totaled, so I quit my job, because I didn't have a vehicle to get there. I never paid back the loan; I figured, fuck it, no car, no loan. Then I got a job as the front-desk receptionist at a hair salon right down the street from my house so I could walk to work.

In the pileup, an elderly lady was slightly injured but wound up being okay. No one could really determine the cause of the accident, but in the paper the next day, it read that a young girl had caused it. I was never charged with anything, but I was very pissed off, because I didn't believe I had been the cause. Then again, I guess I was in denial about a lot of things at that time.

THIS PARTICULAR NIGHT WAS NO DIFFERENT—I was drunk and behind the wheel. I was flying down the highway with the music blaring. I was attempting to fix my makeup in the rearview mirror as I began to swerve toward the passing lane. I felt a quick hard jolt and heard a crashing sound as I moved into the passing lane.

My car began to swerve harder to the left but I quickly regained control. I was startled and looked in the rearview mirror to see a glimpse of a white car bouncing into the guardrail.

I didn't stop.

I just kept driving.

I wasn't sure what had just happened, but I was pretty sure I had hit the other car. But I didn't stop, I kept driving, and when I got to the party and got out of my car, I saw white paint on the side. I went inside and proceeded to get even more smashed than I was already and later drove back to the bar. Just another drunken night on the town.

ABOUT A MONTH AFTER THE BIRTHDAY PARTY, I was planning to attempt what other people would consider a normal Saturday night—"normal" meaning I wasn't going to party or do drugs. I had to work a double shift the next day, and I realized that I needed to start being more responsible with my life. I made plans to go to dinner with my parents, whom I had barely seen during the three months I was living at the bar. I had plans for my best friend and her sister to come over afterward.

I was determined that Saturday would be a different day—maybe I could be normal. In the back of my mind I always knew that I could do and be more. I just kept slipping and could never really get a grip.

I met my parents at a restaurant and was nervous. I didn't have much to say to them and was worried they would see the terrible shape I was in. I got all dressed up and attempted to look pretty. I put a skirt on, and it almost fell off my tiny hipbones. I had been wasting away to nothing, and none of my clothing fit well.

I was edgy at dinner, and when my dad ordered a glass of wine, I thought it would be a good idea for me to also order one. Maybe it would calm my nerves. One glass turned into two, three…and dinner went very well. The edge was gone and my lips were flapping as though I didn't have a care in the world.

I kissed my parents good-night and left the restaurant with a nice little buzz on. I decided I would stop at a store and pick up some things for my friends who were coming over. I purchased a gallon of Skyy vodka, a bottle of mudslide mix, and a bottle of Asti Spumante.

I ARRIVED BACK AT THE BAR, and it was beginning to get packed downstairs. I went right to my apartment, and my friends arrived. We smoked some pot and began drinking the mudslides. Before I knew it, both the champagne and the mudslides were gone and we were fucked up.

We decided to head down to the bar, which was now packed. We hung out and I drank four Amstel Lights and did about five Jell-O shots. I was loaded at this point and lost track of my friends. It was getting late, and I was wandering around the bar looking for someone who I knew would sell me some crack.

I finally found the chef in the poolroom playing pool. I approached him and placed my usual order. I told him to meet me in my apartment in an hour and gave him $100. I found my friends and said good-bye to them and proceeded upstairs. The chef arrived with ten bags of crack and we started smoking. But with each hit I took, it was as though I couldn't get high enough, and I was getting frustrated.

The crack didn't numb the pain like it usually did, and I started to panic inside. I didn't let on to the chef that I was panicky; I just kept trying to get high enough with him, but we ran out of bags, and I never reached a high that was strong enough to ease my pain. My head was spinning in a million directions and I could barely breathe. It was around five in the morning, and we were broke and out of drugs.

I told him I wanted to go to bed and that he should go. He looked at me like he could see through my eyes that I was not okay inside. He asked if he could stay, but I said no, that I needed to be alone. I walked him to the door, and I could see fear in his eyes. He asked me again if I was okay, and I simply said yes. I told him I loved him and thanked him for being such a great friend.

He stared at me oddly and left.

I CLOSED THE DOOR and slipped the chain on. I knew what I was about to do. I was done, exhausted, and I didn't want to live anymore. I couldn't deal with the pain, and I couldn't stand the life I was living, the drugs and alcohol.

I went into the bathroom and opened the medicine cabinet. I took all the medicine I had there, NyQuil and Benadryl tablets. I took them all, more than twenty pills. On my way out of the bathroom, I grabbed my pink razor with daisies on it and broke the blades out of the plastic casing. I discarded the pretty daisies in the trash.

I went to the kitchen, took the bottle of Skyy vodka from the refrigerator, and went into my bedroom. Very methodically, I gathered photos of my family and placed them all around me on my bed. My head was beginning to spin from the pills but I had a level of consciousness that to this day I still cannot explain.

I held the razor to my wrist and began to cry. As the tears splashed down onto my leg I pressed the razor against my flesh and sliced into my wrist. I didn't feel any pain, and as the bright red blood flowed out, I felt free.

I opened the bottle of vodka I had bought to share with my friends earlier that evening and drank straight from it. I drank and cut and drank and cut. This went on for hours. I sat bleeding all over myself and my bed. I had my mother's rosary with me, the one her mother had given her. I was never a religious person, but for some reason this old rosary meant a lot to me. I felt a deep connection to my mother and my grandmother when I held it.

I held it in my blood-soaked hands and thought, "This is it, I am dying, and it is okay. I am ready and I want to die." I had given up all hope. I truly believed I was supposed to die in that moment. I held the rosary tightly and tried to recite the Lord's Prayer, one of the only prayers I knew.

It was imbedded in my head from the little experience I had going to church during my life. I started out, "Our father who art in heaven, hallowed be thy name. Thy kingdom come, thy will be done, on earth as it is in heaven. Give us…" And then I got stuck. I forgot the words.

I couldn't remember what came next.

I got very frustrated and yelled into the air, "Goddammit, what comes next?

"I want to die. This is what I want!

"What is the next line?"

I grew more and more upset and started to cry harder. I kept trying to get it right, but to no avail. My memory was blank. It was as if God were saying to me, "Oh no, my dear, you will not use me as a scapegoat for your weakness. You're on your own."

AT SOME POINT MY ROOMMATE, CARRIE, came home and I walked out into the living room and sat down on the couch. My wrists were bleeding everywhere as I proceeded to light my last cigarette. She looked at me and looked at my wrists and exclaimed, "Storm, what are you doing? What did you do to yourself?" She was wearing her white nurse's uniform to go to work.

I looked at her and said, "Don't worry about it. I am fine." She looked at me and asked if I wanted her to call an ambulance. I said, "No, just let me die. I don't want to be here anymore. I am tired of trying."

She looked at me, and I continued to talk. "You can have everything in the apartment; take everything." I had purchased new furniture, a new TV, and a new stereo with my mother's money. I said, "I do need you to do something for me."

And she asked, "What?"

"Go downstairs and get me a pack of cigarettes." It was like my last wish or something—how pathetic. She kept looking at me and said okay. She went downstairs and purchased two packs of cigarettes, came back upstairs, handed them to me, then turned on her heel, and walked out the door.

She left me there to die. She never said anything to my boss downstairs, from whom she had just purchased the cigarettes. She just left.

I WENT BACK INTO MY BEDROOM and started cutting my wrists more. I had cut so deeply into my right wrist that I could see a gap forming and it was aching. I kept drinking, knowing that the more I drank, the thinner my blood would become and the quicker I would bleed out. I finished the bottle of vodka and was still bleeding badly.

At some point I picked up the phone and called my parents. It must have been around two in the afternoon. I was supposed to be downstairs working but never made it, and no one came looking for me. The phone had rung several times, but I ignored it. I left my parents a message saying something like I loved them and please don't be mad at me. The last thing I remember is lying down on the bed, and everything went black once again.

I heard a loud bang and slowly opened my eyes. My head was swirling, and the room was spinning all around me. I tried to raise my head, but it was too heavy, so I just stared at the ceiling. I saw my brothers rushing into my room. They were yelling at me and at each other but I didn't know what they were saying. Jimmy picked me up and cradled me in his arms as he looked in horror at my bed and my wrists. There was blood everywhere. I glanced down to see the pool of blood I was sleeping in. He wrapped a towel around my wrists and looked at me with such fear in his eyes. I stared blankly back at him. I was so out of it. He carried me downstairs through the bar. I remember seeing people everywhere, and they all stopped when they saw us. They looked at me with pity as my brothers took me out to their car.

BRIAN AND JIMMY RUSHED ME to St. Luke's Hospital, the same place my mother had died three months before. Dad and Pat were already there. I remember the doctors saying they couldn't stitch my wrists up because the cuts had been open too long. They wrapped my hands, and I blacked out again. The next thing I knew I woke up in a little room on a small cot. The room was all white and bare. I looked down to find bright white gauze wrapped tightly on my right hand and a splint on my left hand holding my wrist to my hand. Something was different. I felt hope. I can't explain where it came from, but it was as if my eyes had opened to another world, my vision was different. I felt hopeful that I was going to be okay. The doctor came in and said I was a very lucky girl to be alive. And for the first time in my life, I believed it.

21

Driving to Detox

I STAYED IN THE MENTAL WARD of St. Luke's Hospital for a couple of days until the doctors could find me a bed in a rehabilitation center. The psych ward is not really a place anyone wants to be. There are a lot of sick people in the world, and I feel that I have met many of them. Scattered throughout barrooms and randomly on the street, they appear harmless. But when you have several of them lined up in hospital rooms on one floor, with nowhere to go but a small smoking room where everyone sits with no one to talk to but each other, it can make any person want to scream. There were people who had schizophrenia, who had multiple personality disorder, or who wanted to kill themselves. No doubt, I belonged there, too—after all, I had just taken a razor blade to my wrists. But I wasn't insane. Well, maybe I had some temporary insanity, but I certainly was not certifiable by any means. I like to think I was suffering from a chemically induced insanity caused by lots of vodka and crack cocaine.

The hospital had a social worker come into my room to assess me. Ironically, the social worker had been my very first counselor when I went to the AA group. She talked to me about going to a drug and alcohol rehabilitation program. I just nodded my head yes and said I would try it. At this point, I had nothing to lose and really nowhere else to turn. When we were done, she looked at me and asked if I had ever finished anything in my life. I thought quietly for a moment and realized that I hadn't. One of my greatest fears was my own imperfection, so out of fear of failure, I never finished anything. It was easier to give up than to try to succeed. She looked at me and said, "Well, you are going to rehab for thirty days. Finish that."

I REMEMBER LEAVING THE HOSPITAL and feeling very different, changed in some way. I had no idea what I was about to embark upon, but for the first time in my life I was hopeful, and I just knew, somehow, intuitively knew, that everything was going to be okay. It seemed almost impossible that just seven days earlier, I wanted to die and almost did. The dark, lonely pit in my stomach seemed to dissipate. Now there was this tiny spark, a little light that was faintly glowing in its place. It felt good, warm, and safe. I felt so new, like I was wearing a protective armor. It was like the feeling I had when my mother died, as though something was surrounding me and protecting me.

A driver pulled up to the hospital and picked me up to take me to rehab. I was heading to White Deer Run in Allenwood, Pennsylvania, somewhere in the middle of nowhere, I was told. The location didn't matter much to me; I was simply relieved to be leaving the hospital's psych ward.

I had no idea what to expect, other than that I was about to start a whole new chapter in my life. I wasn't sure what life would be like without drugs and alcohol. They were my crutches for so long, confidantes, always there to help me take the edge off, to transport me directly out of reality into the realm of "safety," or insanity, as some would call it. How would I manage without them? Even as I asked myself this question, I quietly just knew that I would never need them again. That inherent knowledge gave me a greater sense of peace than I had ever felt before. It was intoxicating in a whole new way.

THE DRIVER TOLD ME WE HAD TO STOP at another house to pick up some guy. I found it amazing that this was actually someone's job: picking up psychos, drunks, and druggies at various hospitals and homes to take them to rehab. I wondered what kind of liability insurance he had. This was one high-risk delivery service. I imagined him dropping us off at rehab with a clipboard in one hand and a pen in the other. "I have a delivery for White Deer Run. Let's see, you ordered two crackheads, a heroin junkie, and an alcoholic. Please sign here."

The guy we picked up looked really rough, like he had been up for several days, and as he climbed into the backseat, he clearly smelled like it, too. I introduced myself politely and as I began to slowly judge him in my mind, I became keenly aware of the glaring white bandages on both of my wrists. My judgment quickly halted, and I felt horrible. I think this is what they call humility. He wasn't the one who was just released from the psych ward; I was.

He was very quiet, but halfway through the ride, he asked the driver to stop. He looked over at me, giving me a look that I knew instantly. There was a craving in his eyes, an invitation to get high. He arched his eyebrow and asked, "Want one last high?" I thought about it for a minute. I imagined my lips on the pipe, slowly inhaling the toxic, thick smoke one last time. In my head, I was saying yes, but when I opened my mouth, I said, "No, thank you." He shrugged and got out of the car. I sat there with my mouth gaping open and thought, "What the fuck did I just say? Did I seriously just say 'no, thank you' to crack? First off, who says 'no, thank you'? Me, I guess. I say 'no, thank you' to crack now. Me and Nancy Reagan. Wow." I was amazed. It was that sense of hope inside of me that pushed aside the want, the desire, and the need. They were gone, and I seriously didn't want the drug. I pictured him in the bathroom, hitting that glass pipe with all his might, knowing this was going to be the last hit he would ever take, well, at least for the next thirty days.

The driver didn't seem fazed by this at all. I guess it was common for him, and as my eyes met his, he must have read my mind, because he simply said, "Hey, it's not my place to get in the way of an addict getting his last fix." It made sense to me, but I was happy I didn't have the desire or compulsion to join him. That desire had somehow been lifted from me seven days earlier. That had been it for me; I no longer felt the urge to self-medicate. I lit up a cigarette, though. I couldn't even think of giving those up.

As I took my last couple of drags, the guy came out of the bathroom. As we crawled into the back of the car, I could smell the familiar stench of crack smoke on the guy. As it hit my nostrils, they flared, and my skin began to crawl. As it filtered through my nose, my memory flashed back to my last night, my last high. As though in fast-forward mode, images began to plague my mind—hitting the crack pipe, lifting the vodka bottle to my lips, "Our Father, who art in heaven," slicing and dicing my wrists like a child carving a pumpkin at Halloween, pills, lots of pills. My whole body shuddered fiercely at the recall as I physically tried to shake the memories out of my head. I was so ashamed. How could I have done this to myself? What compelled me to go to such lengths to kill myself? And why the hell was I still here, sitting in a druggie delivery car with a stoned crackhead to my right?

I looked down in fascination to my wrists, to the white bandages. The guy noticed me doing this and asked me what happened. My voice was hollow and almost matter of fact when I replied, "I tried to kill myself." He just nodded as if in total understanding. He clearly knew about the ugly black hole; he could relate without really knowing any of the circumstances behind the bandages. He knew. And his simple acknowledgment of my insanity made me feel totally at ease. I wasn't sure why, but I felt okay. The shame that had crept up earlier dissipated a bit as I realized that maybe, for once in my life, just maybe, I wasn't alone.

WE DROVE FOR ABOUT TWO-AND-A-HALF HOURS and I just enjoyed the scenery around me, beautiful mountains all around. It was November and fall was upon us, so leaves were turning vibrant colors all over the place. Pennsylvania may by far be one of the most beautiful states I have ever seen at this time of year. We neared a small town. As we drove, I noticed a liquor store on the side of the road and made a mental note of its proximity to the road that we turning onto. I found it amusing that there was a six-pack shop right next to the road that led up to rehab. I guess the business owner made a smart market-ing analysis before determining the location of his shop. I could hear his rationale to the banker, "Well, you see, I plan to build right next to the rehab up there on the hill. I figure at least half of the bastards are bound to come bar-reling down the hill at some point to escape, so that should provide me a constant stream of clientele." Loan approved. It was quite brilliant, I thought. As we began to ascend a huge, winding mountain road, I mused, "So this is bum-fuck nowhere—I have always wondered where it was."

We climbed up this very long mountain road and finally crested onto a driveway that overlooked several little white buildings. It was dark by then, so I couldn't see too much, but what I saw looked like what I would imagine camp looking like, had I ever gone to camp. Little cabins were scattered throughout the very large clearing. The driver parked the car in front of a white building with a large porch on the front. I saw a couple people scattered on the porch smoking cigarettes, talking, and checking out the car. I imagined they were curious to see who the new residents were.

A woman came out, met us at the car, and welcomed us. She helped us with our luggage. My parents had packed me a bag, but I had no idea what was in it. I could only imagine them having to go back into my apartment for my things, the scene of my crime against myself. When I got word the driver was coming, I called my stepmother at work to tell her. I could hear in her voice she was pained that they couldn't say good-bye to me in person. I would be leaving for at least thirty days to a place unknown, and I had no idea what to expect. I had been warned that I wouldn't be able to talk to anyone for at least the first couple of days.

The woman walked me into the building. There were several people around who checked me out as she walked me onto the porch and into the building. As we entered, I noticed there were old chairs and couches scattered around a rather large room that appeared to be a recreational room. There was a ping-pong table and a couple of other tables and games lining the shelves on the wall. I skimmed the room looking for a TV but didn't see one, nor did I see a phone anywhere.

APPARENTLY, EVEN THOUGH I HAD JUST SPENT the last couple of days in the hospital, I was still required to spend at least seventy-two hours in detoxification. I guess it makes sense, since I could have easily gotten high on the way up here with the smelly guy riding next to me in the car. The woman who had greeted me walked me through the room and down a dark hallway lined with doors. These were the detox rooms. She entered one room and motioned for me to follow. Inside was a small bed with white sheets and an end table with a blue book sitting on top that had the words *Alcoholics Anonymous* on its cover. I put my bag on the bed. She told me to change into sweatpants and a sweatshirt they had provided. I wasn't allowed to have my bag or my shoes while I was in detox. This didn't faze me, since I hadn't been able to wear real shoes for nearly a week now. I guess people who may or may not be crazy have a tendency to hang themselves with their shoelaces, so I handed my shoes over to her and she took my bag.

She guided me down another hallway to what looked like a little triage room. A nurse was there. She took my vitals and changed my bandages. I had to wear a brace on my wrist to hold it together while it healed. It was a dingy, tannish-brown brace that looped around my thumb and closed with a Velcro tab across my wrist, like the braces they use for people recovering from carpal tunnel surgery. As the nurse took off my brace and peeled away the white gauze from my wrists, swollen, red slices were revealed. Once again I was faced with the horror that I had become that night in my apartment above the bar. My wrists looked like mauled flesh. I couldn't look at them, but I also couldn't look away. It was as though something forced me to stare at them to not forget what I had been reduced to. The gap on my left wrist was the worst. It was still so fresh that I could see an empty blackish-red space that separated my wrist from my hand. I felt like I was staring right into the black hole I always knew I had, as though I had created a physical manifestation of the black pit that I had always known was deep inside of me.

Maybe that was how I released the final demons from my soul. After all, I was still alive and on a road to some form of recovery. Either way, it was disgusting, and I was incredibly embarrassed. I was appalled that I had done this to myself. I couldn't believe I had cut so deep and still lived. How the hell was I still here, alive? I hated looking at the mess I had made, but I knew I would have to see it at least once a day when they changed my bandages and cleaned my wounds. I guess this was part of my penance, my reminder of what was and what will hopefully never be again. The hopelessness that these wounds represented were to serve as a constant reminder to myself as I began my new journey.

DETOX SUCKED, PLAIN AND SIMPLE. It was boring as hell, and I felt like a caged animal. I wasn't allowed out of the building I was in for seventy-two hours. They fed us there and we sat all day long, smoking and waiting to be medically cleared to enter into the general rehab population. At night I heard people moaning in pain; they were releasing their demons in these small white rooms. I was fine; I had released my demons through my wrists that night above the bar. I had nothing left in me to detox; it was time now to rebuild and regain all that I had lost over the years of self-neglect and victimization. But not these poor bastards. They were in their rooms making noises that I never wish to recall again, pain that comes only from a broken spirit and rotten soul as it is released out of the pores in the form of sweat in the night. The noise echoed through the small hallway. I imagined them balled up in the corners of their rooms sweating profusely and rocking back and forth wishing the pain away. I was grateful that I didn't have to experience that pain. I had had my fill. My night was over.

I REMEMBER STANDING ON THE PORCH on my last day in detox, and there was the guy I came up with in the car. He looked rough, and I could tell he was one of the noisemakers from the night before. It was obvious that, like the rest of us, he had had no sleep. Who could sleep with all the noise, the pain, and the lovely bed checks the staff made every fifteen minutes? As soon as you would attempt to fall asleep, as soon as the noise would simmer down, the door would open and bright light would fill the room while a staff person came in to check to see whether you were still alive.

The guy was pacing the porch with his cigarette. He looked up at me, and his eyes were wild. He was a mess, and I could tell he wanted nothing more than to just get out and get high. I knew instantly that he would not make it here, up in the woods, in bumfuck nowhere, turn left with no dealers around the corner, no bar down the block to curb his craving. And his craving was intense; his disease was dancing around in his eyes. It was clear he was on a mission and nothing would stand in his way.

I knew this look; I understood that craving, the compulsion that is beyond reach to control. Oddly, I had not had that craving yet. It had been over a week since I had drunk or taken a drug—a feat that I hadn't accomplished since the day that first sixteen-ounce beer can hit my mouth, that fateful day when I was twelve.

THAT MORNING, I had my daily humbling bandage change and met with a doctor who immediately put me on the antidepressant Paxil. I had only ever been on a prescription once before but didn't adhere to the medication because I simply don't believe in medication. I was never a big pill popper in my addiction. In fact, the only time I really ever consumed pills was to hurt myself during a suicide attempt.

I took the prescription with haste and assured the doctor that I did not suffer from any depression or other mental disorders. Of course, the doctor just nodded, having probably heard this one a million times, and said that he would re-evaluate me to determine that. I took the prescription, because at that point I was just willing to do anything to be okay, and listening to all these trained professionals around me seemed like the perfect place to start. I guess I had begun to turn my will over to the care of others that morning in the hospital when I awoke to find myself still alive.

A big part of getting sober and being clean is realizing that you are not in control. Control, something I needed, depended upon, and demanded in order to survive for so many years, would be a challenge for me to let go of completely. On this day, I was willing enough to swallow the pill and follow basic instructions. This was a starting point and a very significant one, even though I didn't know it at the time.

22

Feeling a Flicker of Warmth

AFTER I FILLED OUT what seemed like a million forms, admission questionnaires, and medical-history paperwork, it was determined that because of my past history with sexual assault, I would be transferred to the women's unit of the facility. I wasn't so sure how I felt about being around all women. I liked women and always had women friends, but I did have a certain level of mistrust, and there was always so much bullshit and drama that came with being around all women. Plus, I was still so unsure of where I stood sexually with women that after my experiences with them, they just plain scared the shit out of me. Regardless, I was just excited to get the hell out of detox, away from the noises, the small space, the stagnant time, and the guy with the crazy eyes.

A couple days later I found out that the guy left AMA—against medical advice—and ran down the hill, most likely right to the bar we had passed on the way up together. *AMA* and other fun little terms became my new language; words like *powerless*, *love*, and *respect*, to name a few, would be woven into my vocabulary over the next couple of weeks.

As I stepped outside the detox building, I noticed how beautiful my surroundings were. There were large trees everywhere and colorful leaves all over the ground. It was a stunning place actually; it appeared to be very peaceful. If I had been able to articulate the feeling at that moment, *serenity* is probably how I would have described it. But I didn't quite know that word or understand its meaning at that time. I knew the place made me feel calm, and that was a nice feeling.

About five yards from the detox building, the women's unit was a large white building. Its big porch on the front held a couple of rocking chairs and ashtrays. Inside there was a reception area where a tech was sitting. *Tech*, another rehab term, stands for *technician*, the people who aren't quite counselors but were essentially our babysitters. I guess *tech* sounds better than *babysitter*. The techs basically ran the various units of the rehab. They woke us up, told us to get dressed, assigned chores for us, ensured that our chores got done, ran our group sessions, and took us to the main hall for meetings and meals.

The tech in the women's unit began explaining to me all the rules—and there were a lot. No drinking and drugging, obviously. No caffeine. No sex. Lights out at 10 P.M. sharp. Up at 6 A.M. sharp. The no-caffeine rule was going to be rough for me, because I liked coffee and diet Pepsi. I needed coffee in the morning to wake up, and I needed my diet Pepsi during the day to sustain my energy. Learning about this rule was tragic to me, as though someone had taken away my security blanket. They had let me have these items in the hospital. No one had told me when I came here that I couldn't have caffeine. I began to panic a little bit, wondering how I would be able to ignite my brain into action in the morning without the coffee. The tech assured me I would be fine, but I was doubtful.

THE TECH ALSO TOLD ME a package was waiting for me. I hadn't been able to see what was in the bag my parents had packed for me either, which was sitting with my new package. Someone from detox had apparently brought the bag over for me. I was really hurting for basic needs like my favorite shampoo, cigarettes, clothing, perfume, hair products, and makeup. I hadn't had makeup for days and was feeling very ugly walking around without my face on. After all, my makeup and hair were my identity in so many ways—who was I without them?

The package was a box from my parents. As I picked it up, I felt like a kid at Christmastime with all the excitement and curiosity of what the contents could possibly be. The tech told me she would need to look through everything first to make sure there wasn't anything that would violate the rules. I assured her I was pretty sure my parents wouldn't sneak in a bottle of Absolut vodka or a crack baggie for me. She blew off my humor, saying, "It's protocol, honey. We gotta search everyone's stuff before we can allow you to have it."

I felt slightly violated but shrugged it off and handed her the box of goodies, feeling pretty confident that there would be no contraband in my things. As she searched through them, I saw some of my clothing, a toothbrush, my hairbrush, my personal things, and I immediately felt better. I had a connection to my life, to my identity. She held the items up and looked inside my shoes, unfolded the clothing as if waiting for a crack pipe to fall to the floor. I kept looking at her with my smug "I told you so" face, until she removed my perfume, my hairspray, my mouthwash, and the nice new package of lighters my parents had kindly put in the box for my carton of Camel cigarettes. I immediately got pissy with her and demanded to know why these items were being removed.

I don't like authority and I really didn't like being told what I could and what I could not do. "I am an intelligent adult who can take care of myself, and if I want my things, I should be able to have my things," I told her. "What does perfume have in it that could possibly be considered against the rules?"

She politely informed me that I was to have nothing with aerosol, alcohol, or any lighters of any kind. I just looked at her with a blankly cocky stare that I am certain she had seen before. She explained further that people had a tendency to drink items like mouthwash or perfume because of the alcohol content, and people can huff cans with aerosol to get high from that. I knew about the whole aerosol deal, although huffing was never my thing. I always thought it was pretty stupid to sit around with Lysol cans trying to get high. The lighters were taken as a safety measure for everyone: safety from ourselves so we wouldn't burn ourselves, and safety for them so we couldn't get really pissed and burn the place down. (We were allowed to use the lighters only during our smoke breaks.)

Now don't get me wrong—I had done stupid shit in the hopes of getting high, simply because I had heard somewhere you could get a buzz from it. Of course, these tactics never worked. Once when I was thirteen, my friend Alex and I were sitting around Richard's house bored out of our minds, because we had just skipped school and didn't have any drugs. Richard was working and wouldn't be home for hours. So as we sat drinking beer, we decided to try all the stupid things that we had heard about that would get a person high—you know, the stupid urban myths that permeate the walls of most high schools. First, we took a cigarette and some toothpaste. We pushed some of the toothpaste onto the tip of the cigarette and let it dry. After it dried, we tried to smoke it. All it did was add a minty flavor to the cigarette and make it burn in a weird way. We also tried to dry a banana peel in the oven, then pick it apart, and smoke it in a bowl. That didn't work either. It tasted horrible and burned the back of our throats.

But drink perfume—was this woman crazy? Who the hell would drink perfume to get drunk? The tech read my facial expression and simply stated, "Honey, some are sicker than others, okay?" My eyes fell to the floor, and I immediately felt that feeling again, the one I had in the car on the way up here—what was that? Shame? Humility? Either one was an odd feeling for me—any feelings really were still just odd. So I shrugged her off and stared into the distance while she finished her inventory of my things.

She handed me my rummaged package, which in some way made it look a little damaged and made me feel a little violated from her strip-search of it. Regardless, I was excited to have some part of home with me.

THE FIRST THING I FOUND IN MY PACKAGE was a yellow envelope with my name on it. I opened it and immediately recognized my father's handwriting. I loved his handwriting—and knew it well because I had forged it like a million times on school notes and permission slips in the past. The letter read:

Hey Jen,

I hope everything is going well. I know how hard it is to make such a quick decision and such a major change, but I think this was a good move on your part. We put this box together pretty quick, and we know it's not everything you need, but we will send more stuff out real soon. We will be calling to see how you are doing on a regular basis and to find out when we can come up. We are proud of you for trying to improve yourself, and Jimmy and Heather said they are also proud of you. Brian sends his love and hopes everything will work out. I know you can't call for a while, but we will write to you this week, and maybe you'll only be restricted for a short period, but however long it is "We're with you on this." Kim [a bartender who worked in the bar downstairs] gave up a lot of your things, and me, Jimmy, and Brian are going over Monday to clean out the apartment and leave Carrie to come home to 0. Your kitten is having a lot of fun with [Jimmy's cat] Shasa, so don't worry about anything but yourself. Well it's 10:15 P.M. and I have to get up at 5 A.M. to get to Easton by 7 A.M. for some stupid meeting, so I'll close now by saying I love you very much, and Pat also loves you very much, so make the best of this and we will be seeing you real soon.

Love you a bunch,
Dad and Pat

PS: The last word is soon.

I held the letter as tears streamed down my face. I had never gotten a letter from my father, and it made me feel warm inside to see his handwriting on the paper and to know that he was supporting me. After all these years and all the bullshit that I had put this man through, he was still there. Amazing.

I was happy to read that they were cleaning my apartment out so that Carrie wouldn't have anything. I didn't want her to have any of my things after she left me there bleeding to death.

I WAS TAKEN TO MY ROOM, where there were two small single beds; mine was next to a window. The tech told me I didn't have a roommate yet but would by the end of the week. She told me to get settled and be downstairs in five minutes for group. "Group?" I asked, with an odd look on my face. "Yes, you have group every day," she explained. "Tonight we have a speaker coming in to talk to you girls." She handed me a sheet with a schedule on it and told me this was what I was to follow each day unless otherwise instructed. As I looked over the schedule, I was floored. I hadn't had this much stuff to do in one day ever:

6:00 A.M.	Wake-up
7:00 A.M. – 7:30 A.M.	Roll call
7:30 A.M. – 8:00 A.M.	Breakfast
8:00 A.M. – 8:10 A.M.	Medication
8:15 A.M. – 8:30 A.M.	Check-in/Morning meditation
8:30 A.M. – 8:45 A.M.	Roll call
8:45 A.M. – 9:45 A.M.	Lecture
10:00 A.M. – 11:30 A.M.	Group session
11:40 A.M. – 12:30 P.M.	Activities
12:30 P.M. – 1:15 P.M.	Lunch/Medication/Store
1:15 P.M. – 1:55 P.M.	Treatment plan
2:00 P.M. – 3:00 P.M.	Lecture
3:00 P.M. – 3:30 P.M.	Cabin cleanup
3:30 P.M. – 4:30 P.M.	Rest time
4:30 P.M. – 5:00 P.M.	Medication
5:00 P.M. – 5:30 P.M.	Cabin cleanup
5:30 P.M. – 6:00 P.M.	Dinner

6:30 P.M.	– 7:00 P.M.	Group session
7:15 P.M.	– 8:15 P.M.	Twelve Step work
8:15 P.M.	– 8:30 P.M.	Cleanup
8:30 P.M.	– 9:30 P.M.	Tenth Step group session
9:30 P.M.	– 9:45 P.M.	Evening medication
10:00 P.M.		Must be back in cabin
11:00 P.M.		Lights out

I wasn't sure about this place. It was so structured and had so many rules. In my past, I lived with no structure, and if there were rules in place, I promptly broke them. I didn't want to screw this up, but at the same time, was I seriously expected to get up at 6 A.M.? That was when I usually stumbled home.

I MADE MY WAY DOWNSTAIRS to a large room with chairs lined up in a large circle. There were women scattered all over, every age, every race—it was like a melting pot. A couple of women introduced themselves to me. Others just stood and stared me down. I knew this game. I was the new girl—just as I had been so many times in my life when entering new schools and towns—and they were going to intimidate me. I held my head high, put on my cocky "don't fuck with me" face, and sat down. I wasn't going to let them get to me, even though inside I felt more vulnerable than I had ever been in my life. I wouldn't let my face show it. I knew how to handle these bitches—I *was* these bitches. I used that same look to intimidate others in the past, and I sure as hell wasn't going to let these women bother me.

The tech started the group meeting by asking us all to stand up, hold hands, and say the Serenity Prayer. I had heard this at the AA meeting I went to a while back, so I

Blackout Girl

was slightly familiar with it. "God, grant me the serenity to accept the things I cannot change, the courage to change the things I can, and the wisdom to know the difference."

We sat down as she began to introduce the woman sitting to her right. She was a pretty woman in her late twenties, and as she opened her mouth and began to speak, I was captivated. With each syllable, each word, each sentence this woman spoke, I was dumbfounded. She was telling *my* story. I could relate to everything she said—the hopelessness, the fear, everything. For the entire hour she spoke, I sat as though in a trance, hanging on to every word she said, as though they were the first words I had ever heard spoken.

I felt like she was talking directly to me. I couldn't believe it. All this time, all these years, I thought I was so unique. I thought I was the only one who thought the things she was saying and did the things she said she had done. All these years I had thought I was alone. That night I realized that I wasn't alone, and I gained this tremendous feeling of hope inside me that told me I may never have to feel alone again. The flicker of light inside me grew a little brighter and began to extinguish a little more of my blackness. I went to bed that night feeling that warm glow in my stomach.

23

Dumping Shit on the Paper Pile

I T WAS MY FIFTH DAY WITHOUT CAFFEINE, and I thought I was going to die. I was in no mood for this "hold hands and chant" bullshit. I wanted a fucking cup of Starbucks coffee, and I wanted it now!

It was my first full day in the women's unit of rehab, and we'd been awakened at 6 A.M. and gone downstairs by 7 A.M. for roll call. I couldn't remember the last time I'd had to get up so early. I was not a morning person, and without my coffee, I was downright nasty. I had trudged downstairs and slumped into one of the chairs, which were still placed in a circular position. I ignored most of the women around me except for the ones who said hello. I grunted "'lo" back. The tech started the morning meditation again with the Serenity Prayer, and then people read some things from daily reflection books. I didn't really hear what people were reading. I had a hard time concentrating because of the headache I was getting from lack of caffeine.

We then headed to the main cabin for breakfast. At this point, I was perking up a little and had begun to make casual conversation with some of the other women. After asking my name, the first question they always seemed to ask was, "What's your drug of choice?" That was a good question. I liked everything, but I quickly figured it was the crack and alcohol that brought me to my knees and into the hospital, so that became my answer. "Crack and booze," I would reply. A knowing nod of acknowledgment would usually follow. All our meals were held in a larger cafeteria in the main cabin, which was also where we had our group meetings and where the entire population came together for outside speakers, other lectures, and weekend meetings.

After breakfast, we came back up to the women's cabin, and I smoked a cigarette on the porch. Almost every person there was a smoker—it was the only vice we were still able to have. When we weren't in groups, lectures, or meetings, then we were on the porch smoking.

WHEN WE HAD TO GO INSIDE FOR LECTURE and morning group session, we all piled into the same room again and sat in the same circle of chairs. The tech picked up a roll of toilet paper from under her chair and held it out in front of her. She informed us that we would be doing an exercise in airing out our shit. I had no idea what she was talking about, and to be honest, she sounded half crazy. She went on to say that we were to think of something that we did in our past while drinking or drugging that we were ashamed of and say it aloud as we ripped off a piece of the toilet paper. After we said it out loud, we were to walk into the middle of the circle and dump the paper in the middle of the room.

I thought to myself, the only shit around here is what this tech is full of. Did she actually think people were going to do this? That we would open up and talk about the bad things we did in our past? Fuck that. I didn't know these women, and I was not about to open up and start dumping out my garbage to total strangers.

The girl next to the tech took the toilet paper and started us off. I was totally uncomfortable and shifting back and forth in my seat. The girl slowly ripped off a piece of the white toilet paper, then walked into the middle of the room and said quietly, "This is for selling my body for heroin." She gently let go of the piece of toilet paper, and we all watched it sway back and forth in the air as it found its way onto the floor. The girl smiled slightly and seemed to be relieved as she turned on her heel and walked back to her seat. She passed the toilet-paper roll on to the next woman, who did the same. "For leaving my children alone to go get high," she said, and another piece of white toilet paper landed on the floor next to the first one. One by one, the women got up, told their deepest, darkest secrets, and left them in the middle of the room in a pile.

I was in awe of the honesty that surrounded me. Some of the women were smiling, and it was clear they were proud of themselves; others were sobbing quietly, and others not so quietly, but they all seemed okay with sharing these emotions. No one looked that uncomfortable. In fact, they comforted each other as the exercise progressed.

I was not used to sharing feelings. In fact, I didn't really know how to share feelings, at least not in a productive way. I knew how to have inappropriate outbursts, but beyond that, my experience with feelings was that they were to be avoided and masked at any given opportunity. I was amazed, and as the roll of toilet paper slowly made it around the room in my direction, I began to squirm in my seat even more. What the hell was I going to say? How could I share my secrets with these strangers? Wouldn't they judge me?

THE PILE IN THE MIDDLE OF THE FLOOR grew larger and larger. To the naked eye it was just a pile of white toilet-paper sheets, but to those in the group, it was a pile of shit, a pile of all the shit we had done to get high, all the horrible ways we had sold ourselves, betrayed ourselves in the effort to get high. It was a mountain of all our nastiest mistakes and most horrific acts.

As the paper came to me, I grabbed it and then just stared at it for a moment. As I felt the soft white roll in my hands, my mind raced. I was paralyzed with fear. As I raised my head to view the pile in front of me, I thought maybe, just maybe I could do this. After all, if these women could share these things, I guess I could share a little bit of my shit.

I took a piece of paper, pulled it away from the roll, and slowly tore it off. I got up out of my chair. My legs felt like they weighed a ton as I made my way to the middle of the room where the pile was. I stood there over the white mountain of mistakes, and when I opened my mouth, I simply said, "For having an abortion." I felt the soft paper slip out of my hand as it glided down to the top of the mountain. It fell gently on top of the other pieces.

I felt a sudden rush of relief and freedom, like I had released that shame from my soul and left it on the pile of shit in the middle of the room. After me, one by one, more women came up and dumped their personal tragedies. That day, we shared things with each other that no one had ever known about us. As we went around the room again, we gained more courage, and women spoke up louder as they acknowledged their past and left it in the middle of the room. By the time we were done, there was no toilet paper left on the roll, and the pile in the middle of the room was huge.

It was incredible to see. A pile of all our worst night-mares laid down before us. I felt good, cleansed in some way. The tech said that this is what we were here to do, to come up to the mountain, to dig deep down within our souls, rid ourselves of all the bullshit, all the bad stuff, to dump it all out on this mountain so that we can walk away free from our baggage.

IT WAS A GREAT ANALOGY, and it made immediate sense to me. That pile of paper lying on the floor represented the reasons so many of us drank and drugged. It wasn't about the drink or the drug; it was about the reasons behind them. It was the shame and guilt that made us want to drink and drug in the first place that we dumped onto that floor.

Things began to click in my mind quickly. I realized that to become a better person, to obtain this "recovery" that people talked about, I had to rid myself of my past. The most important thing I learned on that mountain was that secrets will keep you sick. This resonated with me in a profound way. My secrets buried deep inside were the springboards for my abuse. They were the reasons I drank and drugged and harmed myself. If I could rid myself of all of them, then maybe, just maybe, I could be free from this addiction thing one day at a time.

I had to start dumping my shit out on top of this mountain, so that when I left this place, I would leave my baggage there too—I would be free.

THAT IS EXACTLY WHAT I DID. Each day I dove deeper and deeper into my past. I began to feel this sense of excitement and urgency build in the pit of my stomach. I found a willingness inside of me that I never knew and an honesty that was totally unfamiliar to me. I began to write and talk about myself in an honest way. I wrote about the things I was powerless over, like my addiction, my family, my friends, and my past. I wrote about all the things that made my life unmanageable. I wrote and wrote and wrote every day.

I took every word of advice the techs and counselors gave me as though it were a new gospel I was hearing for the first time. I believed what they said, and more than that, I believed in myself that I could make these changes. It made sense to me that to relieve myself of the desire to escape, I had to face all that I tried to run from before. It was painful and at times utterly exhausting. Reliving all the mistakes and dealing with the feelings and emotions that I had never even acknowledged, let alone felt, was the hardest part for me. I had to identify what feelings were and how to express them appropriately to those around me.

24

Learning to Lean

OVER THE NEXT DAYS AND WEEKS, I did everything I was told to do. I read my *Alcoholics Anonymous* book, I began to keep a journal of my feelings, and I listened to the techs and my counselor. I began to enjoy getting up early and actually seeing a full day to its end in a normal fashion. I loved the group sessions we had and began looking forward to them. As some of my issues would come up, I would be anxious to share them in group because I knew others would relate.

On certain days we went to the main hall where we were able to mix with people from the other units in the center. The White Deer Run center had a unit for people with a dual diagnosis, which are those who had addictions and other mental health issues, a youth unit for those under the age of sixteen, a coed unit for those without sexual assault issues, and a men's unit just like the women's. I learned that some people were there voluntarily, like myself, and others were court-ordered to be there as part of an alternative sentence to incarceration. It was easy to determine who was there because they wanted to be and who was there because they had to be. There was an openness and vulnerability to those who wanted to be there and a toughness to those who were clearly still unsure or downright defiant about their stay.

Each week we would all pile into the main hall for meetings. At my first meeting, the tech who was running the meeting told us to look around closely at each other. He said that in a year only two or three of us would still be sober and several of us would be dead. I watched as people looked around, some with fear in their eyes, some just laughing it off, and some—only a very few—with the same determination in their eyes as I had. I knew I would beat the odds. I would be alive, and I would be sober. I knew in the depths of my soul that I would make it. I don't really know why I knew this, but I did. I had spent my life being a victim to the countless events that unfortunately unfolded into my life, but no more—from this day forward, I was a survivor. I had become a survivor the moment I woke up in that hospital bed alive.

ONE TIME IN GROUP THERAPY, I WAS TALKING about Matthew, a cute guy from the dual-diagnosis unit who had begun flirting with me whenever I would see him in the main hall. I had developed quite the little crush on him. After all, he was beautiful to look at, and it made me feel good when he smiled at me. He was a fun distraction, and that day he had passed me a note to meet him behind the building after chores. I thought this was a good idea. Why not?

As I expressed my crush in group and told about the note I had received that day, I could tell immediately that I had said something wrong. Everyone in my group had amused expressions on their faces. My counselor grew a little angry with me. She asked me if I thought it was appropriate or productive to be fixating on this guy

I didn't even know while I was in rehab trying to save my life. She asked me if I really thought that distracting myself with some guy was going to help me deal with my issues. She said if that was what I was there for, I was to leave now, pack my things, and get off the mountain.

I was pissed off. Who was she to judge me or get angry with me? I was working my ass off, taking suggestions, writing in my journal, speaking up in group. What the fuck? Why couldn't I flirt with a guy? I was an adult. I could do whatever I wanted to do. My counselor looked ashamed of me and simply asked me if I really thought it would be in my best interest to go and meet this guy I didn't know behind a dark building at night. I was frustrated because it did make sense to me. Why not? How could this simple act really harm me? He liked me and that felt good. But as I sat there trying to defend myself, it became abundantly clear that my way of thinking was fucked up.

I panicked. What was I thinking? Why did I think this was okay? Why was everyone looking at me like I was nuts? Why did I immediately want to go meet a guy I barely knew just because he showed interest in me?

My hands started to perspire, and my head was spinning. I began to feel closed in and was having trouble breathing. I was in the middle of a full-blown panic attack. My counselor put her hand on my back and led me through some breathing exercises. I finally calmed down enough to burst into tears. I collapsed into the arms of my counselor and sobbed as my mind began to slowly unwind. It became clear to me that my thinking was not right. What I thought was a good idea was in fact dangerous. This guy was just another distraction for me to keep myself from dealing with my own issues. It was an old pattern for me to immediately assume that just because a guy gave me attention, that I must immediately give it back.

As I expressed this, a tremendous amount of fear overcame me. Could I not trust my own thinking? If I couldn't trust my own thinking, then I must be insane, right? My counselor just looked at me and smiled. I noticed that others in the group were smiling and chuckling under their breath as well. I glared at them with disgust. "What the fuck is so funny?" I yelled. My counselor said, "Honey, you have just had a huge breakthrough."

Breakthrough? My ass! I had just confirmed that I am certifiably insane. If I could not trust my own thinking, then what could I trust? I had always relied on my own thinking. My counselor began to laugh and said, "Honey, your best thinking got you here—don't you see that?"

"Bitch," I thought. As I slowly began to plot my vengeance upon her in my creative little head, it dawned on me that maybe she had a point. Maybe I couldn't trust myself as much as I thought. After all, I was the one stuck up on some mountaintop in bumfuck nowhere with Ace bandages on my wrists covering self-inflicted wounds. Okay, so maybe she had a point. Bitch!

I WENT TO BED THAT NIGHT with a pounding headache, which at this point was par for the course from lack of caffeine and from the emotional upheaval I began to experience on a daily basis. All I did was cry in this freaking place, and that night was no exception. I lay in bed sobbing, thinking about what had happened that day in group. I began to analyze my decisions and began to realize that maybe my ideas weren't always the best ideas. I was scared. I had always relied upon myself, and now I could not even trust my own thinking.

This place was making me feel crazy, and I was starting to think that I had made a mistake by being there. I began crying really hard, and my stomach was starting to hurt from gasping for little bursts of air in between sobs.

Suddenly, I felt a calm enter the room. My eyes were closed but I sensed an indentation on the corner of my mattress, as though someone had just sat on the edge of my bed. I knew this was crazy, because I knew I was alone in my room. I was too afraid to open my eyes. I just lay there continuing to cry until I felt a smooth, gentle feeling move across my head. The feeling kept repeating, a gentle stroking across my head as though someone were gliding a hand over me. I felt at ease, calm, and completely peaceful. I was overwhelmed with love and peace around me. In an instant, I recognized the feeling. It was the same feeling I had after my mother died in my arms.

It was my mother who had come and sat down on my bed, who was stroking my head and making me feel better. I reveled in the feeling for a few moments and then opened my eyes. The feeling immediately left me and the stroking stopped, but I was left with the knowledge that she had been there. She had come to let me know that everything was okay. Whatever happened in my room that night made it easier for me to sleep. I woke up the next day to find myself once again willing to work on myself. I let go. I gave up trying to control things and began to listen to those around me.

THE ONLY OTHER TIME I had ever spent Thanksgiving dinner without my family was when I was broke in Maryland and my dad called his credit card into a local restaurant for me and my roommate to eat dinner. We drank most of the dinner back then. This year, I was spending Thanksgiving in rehab, which was a very sad experience. I went through the cafeteria line like I had three times a day every day since I had been there, but today it was just much sadder than usual. All of us were missing our families and feeling sorry for ourselves. The usually loud cafeteria was oddly quiet as we all ate our nasty processed turkey and lumpy mashed potatoes.

I knew that this would be the start of many very different holiday memories for me. Usually Thanksgiving had been a big drink and drug fest for me. The Wednesday before Thanksgiving had always been a huge drinking night for me and all of my friends, mainly because all our college friends were home for the first time, so we would hit the town hard. I couldn't remember the last Thanksgiving dinner I had eaten when I wasn't brutally hungover or still intoxicated at the dinner table.

While eating a slice of pumpkin pie that tasted more like plastic, it dawned on me that I was never going to drink again—like never ever on holidays, no wine with meals, not at weddings, nothing. It was an overwhelming feeling of fear and remorse. I loved to drink. How would I function in the real world without drinking?

I got really freaked out and shared about it in group that night. Thankfully and as usual, I wasn't the only one feeling that way. We all shared about how hard it was to be in rehab over Thanksgiving and not with our families. The tech reminded us that we would most likely be high if we were home anyway, so what good would we be to our families?

She spoke about "grieving the drink and drug." This was something I hadn't thought of until that day. She talked about how our drinking and drugs were like our best friends, and now that we had put those things down, there was a certain level of mourning that we needed to do to let them go. That made sense to me. Not all of my drinking and drugging times were bad. They didn't all result in trauma, suicide attempts, or death. I had to grieve my loss and realize that my life would be very different from this point forward. In order to move forward it was crucial to dig up our past and talk about the things we had done; however, we were encouraged not to glamorize our past. It was easier to talk about all the nights when we partied hard and had a blast. It is always easier to remember the best times and bury the worst times.

REHAB WAS ALL ABOUT RIDDING OURSELVES of our past and about not keeping secrets. We were told often, "Our secrets will keep us sick." This was the most important thing I learned there. I spent countless hours retrieving memories that I thought were buried deep inside. I would dredge them up in my one-on-one therapy sessions and in my group sessions. I began to get very comfortable with the women in my group. We had a bond that was so rare, so unbreakable, and it made me feel safe for the first time in a long time. I can't explain it, but there was a level of trust and ease with these women that I had never felt with anyone in my life. Even though we were all so different, with different backgrounds, ages, races, and experiences, we all shared this common thread—a common bond of addiction—as women in addiction.

As women, our experiences were vastly different from men's. We were forced to use our bodies in ways that men could never begin to understand. We walked around with shame and guilt that ate at the very core of our beings. And on that mountain, when we shared freely of those experiences, for the first time in our lives, we were able to find comfort and acceptance in each others' eyes. We could see the same pain in each other, we were reflections of one another, and it made us feel safe. We only spent thirty days together, but in those thirty days we gave each other more than any of us had ever received in any long-term relationship we ever had.

With the women up on that mountain, I built a trust that I had never known before. I had very messed-up views of how women should treat one another because, let's face it, my role models hadn't been the best. I was lucky to have my stepmother, because she provided me with some balance in that area, but it was still hard to undo the seventeen years of verbal abuse I'd experienced before she met me. All that changed on the mountain, though. I grew very close to these women, and when it came time for one of them to leave, it truly broke my heart.

WE HAD A RITUAL WE WOULD CONDUCT the night before one of us was to leave. We called it a sing-out. We would pass around the person's *Narcotics Anonymous* or *Alcoholics Anonymous* book, and everyone signed it like a high school yearbook. Then we would gather around in a circle with our arms around each other and place the person or persons in the middle of our circle and sing "Lean on Me."

I have always loved to sing. I would sing in the shower, in my car at the top of my lungs. Singing was a huge part of my life—although the only time I sang in public was when I was drunk enough to get up the balls to sign up for karaoke. People always told me that I had a nice voice, but I never felt comfortable enough to sing in front of anyone unless I was totally hammered. In rehab, I learned how to sing around others, and when we would do the sing-outs, people asked me to start. It felt amazing to open my mouth up and let it all out freely. I didn't worry about what the other women thought, because it felt so good to just belt out the tune.

We meant the words in that song. And even though we each knew we would probably never see each other again, we knew deep down we could still lean on each other. When we were afraid, we would just have to close our eyes and remember the strength of our group and the memories of our time on this mountain.

25

Living Halfway and Beyond

WHEN IT CAME CLOSE TO MY TIME to leave the women's rehab unit on the mountain, I was a bit nervous. I wasn't sure where I was going to go. The counselors and the techs stressed avoiding people, places, and things from our old life. I knew I couldn't go home; I wanted nothing to do with that place. I took the advice of my counselor and agreed to go to a halfway house for women in recovery in Lancaster. My last night, as tradition, they sang "Lean on Me" to me and signed my book. I have never been to camp in my life, but I would like to think this was my "camp" experience. I made amazing friends and found incredible strength, trust, and peace with these women. They changed my life, and I am forever grateful to them. This little group of women touched me in ways they and I will probably never truly understand. They aren't my family or even lifelong friends, but they had a greater impact on me than anyone else ever had.

I didn't enjoy the halfway house experience as much as I had enjoyed rehab. It was awkward being thrust into yet another environment of all women, especially after the incredible experience I had had at rehab. It just felt like nothing could compare to the bonds I formed there. I was on what people in the program refer to as a "pink cloud"— a euphoric feeling that many newcomers to sobriety experience. It leaves as quickly as it comes, and when I got to the halfway house, I fell hard off my "pink cloud." I tried to be open-minded, but the halfway house was very different.

First, it was an actual house in the middle of Amish country in Mountville right outside Lancaster. I had never really been to Lancaster, so I knew nothing around me. It was a good move, because there was no way I could go back to Allentown. I just knew in my heart that I would struggle deeply there. Allentown held dirty people, places, and things around every corner for me.

Second, I had to share a room with two other women. At rehab, I had only one roommate, or none, which was nice. Putting three female addicts in one small room together can have catastrophic results. Personalities often clashed and resulted in screaming matches or downright fistfights. Eventually, though, I made some friends there, and it provided me an opportunity to test living in the real world.

The first couple of weeks, we were not allowed to work and mainly spent all our time in intensive group therapy and individual therapy sessions. We were not allowed any visitors for the first seven days. There were so many rules and so much structure—which was the point. Addicts don't live structured lives, and all the strict rules were in place to get us used to what people in the regular world live by.

There were group levels. I was in a group in which I was to stay for the first six weeks as an adjustment period in a new environment. We were each given a treatment plan within the first seventy-two hours. Mine was as follows:

- Attend a minimum of five Alcoholics Anonymous (AA) or Narcotics Anonymous (NA) meetings per week.
- Attend weekly community meeting on Thursday at 6:30 P.M.
- Attend weekly educational/lecture meetings series as [I was] available.
- Attend a weekly clinical group counseling session.
- Attend all scheduled, individual biweekly counseling sessions.
- Learn social skills via mandatory attendance at all house activities.
- Read *Twenty-Four Hours a Day* book or a meditation book of your choice daily.
- Participate in morning peer group as [I was] available.
- Read from the *Alcoholics Anonymous* or *Narcotics Anonymous* text daily.
- Return all materials and assignments to office by the due dates.
- Make staff aware of all outside appointments/ engagements.

I was given all kinds of assignments, books and articles to read, pamphlets to fill out, and feelings exercises. It was like being in school, really, and before I began using, I had been a good student. I slowly began to rediscover that good student inside of me. I had always loved to read, so I dove right into the texts, read everything I was supposed to, and wrote out all of my assignments with as much willingness and honesty as I could muster on any given day. It was hard, and there were days when I wanted to just give up and leave. There were days when I hated everyone and everything around me, but I learned productive ways to deal with the bad feelings. Writing was one of my primary healing tools. It helped me release the chaos from my head onto a piece of paper. The power of the feelings was taken away if I wrote them down. Here is an entry from one of my journals on a bad day, when my daily struggle was evident:

December 12, 1997

My mind is spinning out of control. I'm feeling so crazy. I hate this disease. I hate that I have no control over my feelings, emotions, thoughts, and actions. I hate that one minute I am happy then sad, then angry, then frustrated—all these feelings at once, and I need to get out of my head and talk, write, express, feel these feelings. People tell me this is normal, but I do not feel normal. Why me? Why can't I have a normal mind and normal life? Am I not deserving? Or am I the normal one and everyone else is fucked up? I am doing something about it. I'm confused, scared, and I feel like a lost child without a mother to guide me through this. People really fucking piss me off here. I hate this world. I'm so powerless! Powerless! I hate my feelings, emotions, anger, hatred! I have no positive affirmations. People get on my fucking nerves and I want to scream.

That was my reality; some days were great and others were utterly devastating. There is a line from one of my favorite movies, *When a Man Loves a Woman*, that I feel sums up this roller coaster of feelings brilliantly. Meg Ryan's character says something like, "That is the fun of all this; it just comes by and hits me like a goddamn freight train." To this, Andy Garcia's character asks if there is a printed schedule so he can plan around her breakdowns. Guess what—there isn't. There is no rhyme or reason for the emotional upheavals recovering addicts have or the feelings that fly through us by the minutes, hours, or days.

I was learning how to process feelings and how to interact with others in a healthy manner. In a house full of women, this was especially hard. We were all struggling on so many levels. One major house rule was that we were to call each other out on our shit. That meant if someone was behaving in a way that was deemed unhealthy, we were to confront her in a healthy manner. If it was something we could work out with the person, then we were to call for a one-on-one session with her. One of our peers would mediate a discussion between the two housemates to resolve a conflict. It usually worked out very well. It was a hard thing to do, because for most of us, confrontation in a healthy way was a foreign concept.

If it was a matter that the entire house—which consisted of about twenty other women—needed to be aware of, we had a bell that we would ring. No matter what time of day or night, if someone rang the bell, everyone was to report to the living room. Usually this was done when someone was really struggling and wanted to leave or was feeling like she wanted to use. Some days the bell rang constantly; other days it was quiet.

I slowly began to gather inner strength and found it easier to identify and discuss my feelings with others. Personal accountability was stressed to us on a daily basis, and collective accountability was a rule. We were to help each other all the time. We had to fill out peer evaluations often in which we would answer questions and make statements about each other, for example, "List five areas of positive change or list three examples of positive assertive behavior" and stuff like that. They were usually helpful, and we all tried to stay open-minded, but at times, they were just annoying. It felt odd having to grade our peers' emotional and behavioral progress. I had to live with these women so I didn't want to be harsh, but at the same time, we were trying to help one another change old behaviors. It was interesting to have others hold me accountable for my actions, and to do that for them. I understood that the purpose was to grow together and see behaviors in others that we may also possess.

I SPENT MOST OF CHRISTMAS AND NEW YEAR'S EVE in the halfway house. I got to go home briefly for Christmas, and that was wonderful—I held my niece and enjoyed my family.

On New Year's Eve at the halfway house, we were all to go to this NA dance. I was nervous about the idea of spending a sober New Year's Eve; I hadn't done that since I was twelve years old. We got all dressed up and headed out to the dance. It was held in a barn. Food and nonalcoholic beverages were served, and a DJ was playing some really good music. People were starting to dance, though many of us from the house were hesitant to do so. I had never danced sober. I didn't think I could. I usually never took to the dance floor in a club until I was good and buzzed, so this was new territory for me. I decided to give it a shot, and as I began to feel the music and move my body, I began to feel incredibly free. I was actually a pretty good dancer. I amazed myself at how easy it was to move with the music without being high. I had a blast that night, dancing my butt off until midnight. When 1998 approached, I was clean, coherent, and having a blast

—three things I had never thought would be possible. I knew inside that this year would be better than any other.

I KEPT IN TOUCH WITH MATTHEW, the guy from rehab. In rehab, I had met him behind the building, we kissed, and we kept writing notes back and forth and later during my stay. It was an old pattern for me to immediately assume that just because a guy gave me attention, I must immediately give it back. Old habits die hard.

They tell you in recovery to avoid relationships for the first year. This is much easier said than done. When you have a group of people getting clean and sober and finally discovering themselves again, well, it tends to bring hormones to the forefront. Many of the girls in the house were having sex or had boyfriends or girlfriends.

The awareness of knowing my actions were not healthy was new for me; however, following that knowledge with the appropriate action was something I hadn't quite mastered. But just questioning my own actions and thoughts was a start. I began to develop a moral compass, but it was new, and some days it just spun around and landed on whatever direction I wanted to go in. Even when I would do something I knew wasn't in my best interest, I began to feel it deep in my gut. Being new to all this, I found it took me a while to start actually listening to those gut feelings and then acting differently. Outside of rehab, Matthew and I wrote to each other every day and talked on the phone as much as possible. He told me he loved me, and I loved the attention he offered me. He was living in State College and invited me to move there to live with him. He lived with his father, and his dad had said I could move into his sister's old room until I got on my feet. It seemed like a good option for me. Matthew was staying clean and sober and had found a great recovery community there. I decided that was where I would go after leaving the halfway house since I really had no other options.

We dated briefly while I lived there, but I quickly realized that a relationship at this point was not a smart move and that he and I were better off as friends. I wanted to approach this sobriety thing right. I found a group of amazing sober people, a great counselor, and a sponsor. I began attending meetings every day. I eventually moved into my own apartment, a little one-bedroom studio that was perfect for me. I had money left from my mother's insurance, which I was able to use for rent and really focus on myself for a while. My parents helped me with bills and rent as much as they could. They were just so happy I was alive and doing well that they were willing to support anything I did as long as it was positive. This support helped me in more ways than I can explain.

I SPENT TWO YEARS IN THERAPY dealing with all my past issues, my mother, my friends dying, the sexual assault, my self-mutilation. I found peace in sobriety. I found a new way of life, but it wasn't easy. I had to dig deep and change everything about who I was, the way I viewed things, and, the hardest part, how I dealt with my feelings. I had never had any tools for how to deal with emotions, so I had never dealt with anything. I spent a lot of time writing and journaling about my experiences and did massive inventories on my past. I was working the Twelve Steps of Alcoholics Anonymous. Doing the Steps meant I made long lists of things I was powerless over, things that made my life unmanageable, anything that would illustrate how drugs and alcohol were in control of my life and damaging to it. This really helped me get to the core of the issues, to see my role, and to see other people's roles in my addiction. It helped me understand that not everything was my fault, that I wasn't a bad person, but I had made bad decisions. I had always been a very intelligent person, but I just didn't know any better. And honestly, it was easier to get high than to attempt to deal with the shit that was running through my head.

I slowly began to rediscover the little girl I had left behind so many years ago. I had grown up so fast and somehow abandoned her on the way. I trudged through so much of the wreckage of my past, and along the way I began to build a relationship with that little girl again. I began to feel like her again, new and innocent in a way that I hadn't felt since I was about eleven years old. It's said that addicts emotionally retard themselves upon the age they begin to abuse a substance. I began to feel like my overachieving, perfectionist self again. The little girl who had dreams and goals and hopes and desires was awakened from the drunken, cocaine-induced stupor in which I had held her captive for so many years.

So now I walked around with this amazing dichotomy inside myself. I was this mature woman who had been through hell and back, who had seen more and done more in my first twenty-two years than most fifty-year-olds have, yet I had rediscovered this innocent little girl inside of me. I now had to figure out how to enable these two vast personality differences to coexist.

I HAD MY UPS AND DOWNS like anyone new in sobriety. But I did what the Twelve Steps taught me to do, which was just to live one day at a time and put one foot in front of the other. I had some really hard days, emotional days when I would cry my eyes out and scream. I stumbled through learning how to appropriately express my feelings, as it was a huge development for me. I made mistakes like most newly sober people do, like misplacing my feelings, going to bars, and trying to still be young, but thankfully I never relapsed. No matter how hard it got, I just looked at my wrists and remembered vividly how hard it had been. Nothing in early sobriety could compare to the despair and desperation of that fateful night, and just running my fingers over my scars helped me to stay sober one more day. I still occasionally would see someone with a drink and, for a brief moment, my mouth would water a bit and it would look appealing, but then I would replay some of my most humiliating and horrifying drunk nights in my head.

We were taught in rehab to expose the disease, so if and when I had even the smallest desire to drink, I was to immediately tell someone and get it out of my head. It did really work. I have learned that I am an alcoholic and this will never go away. I can stay in recovery by being honest and vigilant about my disease, but at the end of the day, I am an alcoholic and addict. My knee-jerk reaction to situations in life has always been to pick up a drink or a drug.

Being sober is a learned behavior that I had to incorporate into my life on a daily basis. I have to be careful not to go backward. It is a daily process, one I will never be totally free from. Somewhere in the *Alcoholics Anonymous* book is this statement: "What we really have is a daily reprieve [from our disease] contingent on the maintenance of our spiritual condition."* I still have to go to meetings, talk to my sponsor, journal my feelings out, and take care of myself.

---

*From *Alcoholics Anonymous*, 4th ed. (New York: Alcoholics Anonymous World Services, 2001), 85.

SEEING AS I WAS LIVING IN STATE COLLEGE, home to Pennsylvania State University, going to college became very appealing to me. I had always been envious of my friends who had gone there, and I knew that was an experience I wanted. My counselor connected me with the Office of Vocational Rehabilitation. The staff there helped me apply for school and also provided me with grant money to pay for it. I had never taken my SATs or anything, so I thought college was impossible. I wrote my essay for admission with passion and conviction, not holding anything back about where I had been in my past and where I was today and how desperately I wanted to go to college. I was accepted at Pennsylvania State University on a provisional basis, got almost all A's my first semester, and went on to earn a bachelor's degree in rehabilitation education.

During my freshman year, I finally came to fully accept my sexuality and came out of the closet. Like any good addict, I didn't just come to some soft understanding of my sexuality. Oh no. I came flying out of the closet like a racing bullet straight into activism for the gay community. I became a strong activist on campus and was involved in several organizations fighting for justice, equality, and civil rights for all. While at Penn State, I learned so much about myself and about the human race. My mind, body, and spirit underwent a dramatic transition. I learned who I was at the core of my being, not who I became when I applied makeup or a certain outfit. I stripped away all that I thought I was, all that society demanded of me, and I became anew.

26

Revisiting Lee

A S I WROTE THIS BOOK, I DECIDED to find out exactly what happened to Lee, the man who violated me when I was twelve. Because I now work in the criminal justice system, I know that as a crime victim I have rights to this information, so I picked up the phone and called Northampton County Courthouse and spoke to a kind woman in the district attorney's office. I explained to her who I was and why I was calling. I told her that I had been sexually assaulted as a child and wanted any information she had on the disposition of the case. She asked me to put my request in writing and send it to her.

I carefully wrote the letter on my agency's letterhead, thinking that might bring me some clout, because I found myself suddenly filled with anxiety and fear. See, the thing about being victimized is that you are never really the same. You can go to countless hours of therapy and find healthy coping skills and write letters to your offender that you then burn and do all the things that self-help books and psychologists tell you to do, but at the end of the day, you are still changed. You still carry an irrational fear that, while walking down the street one day, you will be attacked and sexually assaulted. When you're alone in your house, you have a strange fear that someone will come in and get you again.

These are emotional scars that I carry on a daily basis. Because once someone intrudes upon your sense of personal safety in that way, it is *never* replenished. You never walk totally free from fear. That piece is hard to explain to people who have never been raped or sexually intruded upon. People will tell you that you should move on and let go, or they will look at you in a confused manner and ask you why you aren't just over it already. It is because you are never truly *over* an experience like that. Getting over something means you haven't walked through it, and if you haven't walked through it, you can never truly move on.

Yes, I have moved on, and I walk through it every day in one way or another. I have even reached a place of forgiveness. However, I will never forget, and although most days I walk around feeling unaffected by these events, I carry them with me, sometimes hidden deep inside and sometimes right at the surface. These are my emotional scars; they run under my skin like thread on a multicolored, highly elaborate, handmade tapestry. Each experience is a scar, a thread, and all those threads are interwoven and make up who I am. They are the very fabric of my being. They sometimes rise to the surface when I least expect them. They make me cry at the drop of a hat at some odd time that doesn't really call for tears, or I will feel a rush of anger or fear for no rational reason and have to sort it out in my head before I realize the source of the feeling.

Thankfully, I have learned in therapy that this is normal and in fact part of post-traumatic stress disorder (PTSD). My counselor explained PTSD to me, and we were both sure that I suffer from it as a result of all the trauma

I experienced growing up. I also studied the physical and emotional effects of trauma in my counseling classes at college, which really helped me understand my actions and feelings. Learning about it gave me a name for my feelings and behaviors, and that was comforting. My fears associated with past trauma will never totally go away, but today I have tools to understand my emotional responses and reactions. Additionally, since becoming clean and sober, I have begun to add many more bright, colorful, loving threads of experience to my tapestry.

However, on the day I wrote the letter to request some of my missing pieces of information from that fateful night, some of my ugly, old, tattered emotional scars chose to unravel and made me scared shitless at actually seeing the documentation from the courthouse in writing.

A DAY LATER, I GOT A MESSAGE on my cell phone that the woman had located the files and would send them to me in the mail. I was nervous at the idea that when I walked back into the office, there would be answers there for me that I hadn't had. When I got to work, there was nothing in my mailbox. Around 2 P.M., the mail came and an envelope was dropped onto my desk from Northampton County Court of Common Pleas, Criminal Division. I sat with the crisp white envelope lying on my desk in front of me. I starred blankly at it, not really wanting to open it yet. I pushed it aside and opened the rest of the mail that came in. A coupon for a 10 percent discount at OfficeMax and a couple of other random pieces of mail occupied my mind momentarily, but my eyes kept wandering to that white envelope.

Why was I so afraid to open it? I knew for the most part what had happened, even though there were still lots of blanks in my mind and lots of details missing. I guess the reality of learning some of those details was far too scary for me. It is funny how even after all my therapy and all my knowledge on victimization, I can still find myself in denial or with the ability and desire to not face my past. I slid my letter opener under the white tab of the envelope and tore it open slowly.

Inside was a printout of the recorded actions that occurred in the case against Lee. It showed the date he was arraigned on the charges, the date of the preliminary hearing, the name of the district attorney, and other details. I found it interesting to read, because it filled in some of my blanks, little things like the name of that district attorney, the dates of the criminal proceedings. Simple facts, but they were things I hadn't known before. They filled in small pieces of the puzzle and brought the shattered memory into a little more focus. Somehow these small, mundane facts brought me comfort. It was as though seeing it all in writing made it more valid. I felt empowered with information as the blanks began to fill in around my scattered memories.

As I read down the page, I was struck by something. I noticed the trial dates were continued on several occasions, which I know commonly happens. As I noted the dates, I also figured these continuances were due to the fact that I was in the psych ward at that time. But it was what came next that stopped me dead in my tracks. All the charges were *nolle prossed*, which means that the district attorney's office chose not to prosecute at that time, but reserved the right to refile the charges at another time. The court report went on to list that Lee pled guilty to a charge of criminal attempt rape. He was sentenced to county jail for two to four years effective November 18, 1988. He was to pay $206 in court costs. No restitution was ordered, no other fines or costs assessed.

My jaw dropped and I was utterly speechless. All I could think was "*Criminal attempt*, criminal attempt, my ass. The man fucking violated me." I was furious. My blood began to boil, and I could feel my whole body getting warm as my eyes flooded with fluid that cascaded down my cheeks before I even realized I was crying. What the fuck is this? I threw the paper down. My mind was racing a million miles an hour. I was trying desperately to recall whether anyone had told me of this. My memory was coming up blank. I had been under the impression all my life that this man pled guilty to statutory rape, and now here on this white piece of paper was the truth, the truth that had been kept from me all these years.

TO THIS DAY, I HAVE A HARD TIME talking to my father about things like this, so I rely on my stepmother first as my sounding board. I picked up the phone and called her at work. I asked her if she had ever talked to my father about it, and she said, "No."

I drove home in total disbelief and disgust. I felt so incredibly violated. I knew some of my feelings were irrational, yet I was still feeling them. They were still real in the moment that I felt them. I felt as though I couldn't call myself a rape survivor because he didn't plead guilty to rape, as though the words *criminal attempt* in front of *rape* somehow took that experience away from me. I was so incredibly upset that I couldn't talk about it. It stirred up all those emotional scars that had been stored neatly in their respective places never to be heard from again, or so I had thought.

I felt dirty and I felt betrayed. In some ways, I felt violated again. My memory of what had happened to Lee was taken from me. Why hadn't I been told this? Why didn't my parents fight for me? Why didn't they want to have this bastard convicted of what he really did to me? Maybe I was a bad witness? Maybe I was a bad girl? All those guilt and shame feelings came bursting out of my pores uncontrollably as I drove home barely able to see the road before me, blinded by my tears.

MY FATHER CALLED ME BACK that night and we talked. He said he didn't remember much, that he also had blocked it all out. I guess he has a secret room in his head where he stores bad memories, too.

As the night went on, I began to regain some rational thinking. I know I am not a bad person, and I know that I was messed up back then after this happened. My parents did what I have watched so many parents do in my work every day: They did what they thought was in the best interest of their daughter. To avoid a trial and having to testify yet again, especially after I had tried to kill myself, they decided to let the district attorney plea the case out. Taking that route is so much easier to get it over and done with quickly, and my parents just wanted it over so they could avoid talking about it again and move on.

A part of me really wishes they had not made that choice back then, that they would have let me testify again at trial. But honestly, if it were my child, today, I don't know what I would do. It is hard when you are put in a position in which you have to make a decision on behalf of another person. They tried to do what they thought was right. They couldn't have known the anger or pain it would cause me almost twenty years later.

I am grateful that today we have a kinder, gentler system for children and for rape victims, one in which we empower and encourage women to stand up and step forward, using their voices to reclaim what sexual assault and rape take away. I am honored to be in a position to help women have that choice, a choice that—like the assault itself—was made for me without my knowledge or consent. I urge people who meet a rape victim or know anyone among their family, friends, and colleagues who has been raped to let the victims use their voices if they can. It will give them strength and hope beyond any words of comfort you can offer them. We must believe them and listen to them, even when their words don't totally make sense. Even if their descriptions of the events seem scattered and the facts slightly off, believe in them. I have come to realize from my own experiences that memories of traumatic events don't always flow out of us like pages of a story. They come out broken—much like we do—and it takes patience and understanding to help us put the pieces back together so that it all makes sense.

When you are traumatized, it affects every part of you—your brain, your nervous system, your soul, your spirit, your smile. You often cannot recall the big picture, but you can focus for hours on one small insignificant detail. You can recall a smell but not the source of the smell. Having such fractured memories is an odd experience and makes it extremely difficult to explain it all to someone, because you know it sounds irrational. Even to this day, I am not always comfortable explaining my assaults to people. Even though the majority of my memory is put back together, there are still pieces missing.

I always fear that people won't believe me, that they will say, "Oh, well, she was drunk," "She should have known better," or "What was she thinking, putting herself in all those places?"

Well, guess what? I didn't know better. I wasn't thinking. I was powerless over my disease. I was young and impressionable and insecure and scared. These are not excuses; they are simply the facts. I am not the one to blame, nor is any other rape or sexual assault survivor. It doesn't matter what I do, what I wear, what I say, what I drink—no one has the right to violate my body. No one has the right to touch me without my consent. And I *cannot* consent when I am drunk. This is something that should be taught to every young boy and girl in health class.

Someone who is an adult himself and finds a twelve-year-old child sexually attractive is a sick person who needs to be locked up and given treatment. Someone who sees a drunk girl blacked out on a bed and thinks to himself, "Here is a good opportunity to get laid," is perverse and disgusting.

I am not the one to blame; they are, and in many ways, so is society. Even though times have gotten much better with education and awareness, little boys still grow up with the same messages. They are taught that women are not their equals but are something less and, therefore, can be, and in many ways should be, dominated. We still see advertisements in which women are depicted as animals and sex objects. We still live in a world in which a rape victim comes forward in a high-profile case and the lawyers and the media ask what she was wearing at the time, who she slept with the night before—all questions aimed at making the victim look bad. What about the defendant? What about what he said, what he did, the fact that he forced himself upon a person? Why don't we hear about that? We don't want to believe that some of our cultural "heroes" could be responsible for raping someone. We want to blame the victim, make her a whore, so our image of male perfection isn't shattered.

Very few sexual assault and rape victims lie about what has happened to them. I mean, really think about this for a minute. Why would any woman put herself through the torture that the criminal justice system and the media can inflict upon a rape victim? Who would want to expose her family and herself to the scrutiny of cross-examination and public ridicule that we face? The distrust and humiliation that ensues is often worse than the actual rape itself. This is why we still have so many unreported assaults in this country.

I LOOKED AT THE COURT PAPERS ONCE AGAIN and continued where I left off. Lee served almost three years before being permitted to work at some new work-release facility. He was paroled on June 10, 1991. There was a bench warrant issued for him months later for failure to pay court costs. He was recommitted on a bench warrant and then released once again a couple of days later after paying the fines.

The last line made me sick to my stomach. It listed the bail that was listed at the time of the crime on April 5, 1988, in the amount of $5,000—$5,000 for the rape of a child. How sick is that? What kind of system, what kind of judge only orders $5,000 bail when the offender is charged with rape? I would love to say that today, almost twenty years later, things are different, and in some ways they are, but for many assault and rape victims, this disregard for the victim and for public safety is the status quo.

Thankfully, today we do look at child predators differently. We have creative ways of catching them now, and we air these dirty scoundrels on TV. People are often still shocked when they watch these shows and see men from all walks of life walking into homes expecting to find a young girl they can have sex with. Yet we still question girls and women when they come forward and accuse someone famous or a family member whom they thought they could trust. Why is that? Denial? I have seen so many children come through the doors of my office with hard-core evidence that they had been raped by someone in their family. And I have seen parents and other family members turn their backs on their children out of their own denial and fear. I feel that when you don't believe a child, it is the worse victimization you can inflict upon that child. Children do have great imaginations; in fact, it is one of the greatest gifts and beauties of being an innocent child. I can assure you, however, that if children's images include things like sexual assault and violation of their personal space, it is most likely more than their imagination talking.

We do have better systems in place to protect our children. In turn, all this media hype gives parents a powerful tool: the words and opportunities to talk to their children about these things. When I was twelve, things like this weren't talked about at the dining-room table. They were horrible things you didn't speak of. Today we live in a different world, and parents should be and must be educating their children on how to protect themselves and how to make healthy choices.

For me, for now, this court information about Lee serves as a little piece of closure on this event in my past—closure that honestly I didn't even think I needed until I wrote this book. But again, those are the realities for me. Just when I think I have healed and closed the door on something, a little wedge slips in and keeps it slightly ajar.

27

Dealing Today

TODAY, WITH MORE THAN TEN YEARS OF SOBRIETY, I love my life. I am still growing tremendously and still have so much to learn and do. I have found a new freedom and a new happiness in sobriety. Each day provides a new opportunity and beginning, and I look forward to every sunrise now, because it is the start of new possibilities.

I see it as a gift that I am alive today. I shouldn't have awoken in that hospital bed that morning after my last suicide attempt, but I did. It was a miracle, and I truly feel as though I was chosen by something much larger than I to continue living and to carry a message of hope to others. So many people living with addictions cannot find recovery no matter what they do. I feel truly blessed to be one of the very few to have been able to get sober and maintain sobriety one day at a time for as long as I have. I now know that I have a purpose in life, and as long as I continue to live an open and honest life, I will continue to cherish that gift. I don't always do it perfectly, but that is not the point. It is about progress and living along a spiritual path of continual growth. I try to look at everything as a learning experience and a way for me to personally grow.

I WORK AS THE EXECUTIVE DIRECTOR of the Victim/ Witness Assistance Program in Dauphin County, Pennsylvania, which is essentially Harrisburg and the surrounding areas. I work with victims and witnesses of violent crime. I am able to use my personal experience and pain and channel them into advocacy for others. It is a gift beyond anything I could ever have imagined. I see myself in so many of our clients. I am able to approach clients with a deep level of understanding because I have been there. I have walked their walk.

I remember one of the first cases I worked on with another advocate. It was the case of a twelve-year-old girl who had been raped by a twenty-eight-year-old man. She was me so many years ago, and it was awe-inspiring for me to watch her walk through her pain. It helped me heal in more ways that I can ever explain. It allowed me to see clearly what an actual twelve-year-old girl looks like—she is a baby, a child. I had always envisioned myself as so big at that age, and I think that mispercep-tion enabled my self-blame and self-loathing over my own sexual assault. I thought since I was drunk I must have somehow been to blame. But as I sat in court with this little twelve-year-old girl, I realized she was nothing but a child, and how could anyone find her sexually attractive? It wasn't until that moment that I found a deeper sense of forgiveness with myself, and I owe it to that little girl. She gave me more than I probably ever gave her during those days of her trial.

Of course, I never shared my experience with her. That isn't how it works. When I am working with a client, it isn't about me. It is about that person and his or her pain and suffering. At work, it would be incredibly selfish of me to ever bring up my own pain or suffering.

But at home at the end of a day, I do have to deal with my own pain. I have found healthy ways to channel my energy and release my emotions. To release my emotions physically, I get on the treadmill and run my butt off until all the pent-up energy leaves my body. But sometimes I need a more emotional release, and for that, I take a hot bath and allow myself to feel.

I SLOWLY TURN THE KNOB as warm water runs through my fingers and splashes onto the clean white linoleum. Quickly the water turns hot and steam begins to rise, gently fogging up the mirror and moistening my flesh. I sprinkle muscle-relaxing powder over the water and breathe in deeply. Eucalyptus fills my nostrils and relaxes me as I exhale. The spark of my lighter glides over the wicks of four candles that I placed in the corners of my bathtub. I hit "Play" on my Indigo Girls CD and slowly slide my robe off my weary body. I step into the steam and lower myself into the heat. Inch by inch, I can feel the warmth seep through my skin and soften my tired muscles.

I lie there staring at the ceiling, my mind slowly unwinding from a busy week. Thoughts drift in and out. Did I pay the electric bill? Is there popcorn in the cabinet for my movie tonight? I should call my dad later. I should talk to my niece and tell her how much I love her. My eyes droop and eventually close as I drift off into a meditative state, taking in the various aromas around me, breathing deeply through my nose and exhaling out my mouth. My whole body begins to sweat under the water's intense heat. My heartbeat quickens and my head begins to gently pound. My body trembles slightly as something forms in the pit of my stomach, a knot unraveling inside me, loosening something buried so deep within. My whole body starts to shake, and all of a sudden, like an erupting water main, tears begin to crash onto my cheeks, flowing uncontrollably, cascading down my face, and splashing onto the water below. I am sobbing nonstop as a noise spills from my mouth, a moan that elevates to an outright cry. This noise is the knot slowly unraveling from my stomach up through my throat and out of my mouth. The noise turns into a scream, and I begin crying so hard I can barely breathe, my mind spinning, thinking of love lost, lives changed. I sit up with my arms wrapped around my quivering body, comforting and holding myself.

Leaning over onto the cool side of the tub, I place my head in my arms. I cannot control this. I have tapped into something deep inside, and it is releasing itself like a dam breaking. I am caught up in the ride, and there appears to be no end near. My head is pounding now, and my heart is racing like wild. I weep like this for over an hour, thinking of all the pain, hurt, and death I have witnessed in my life.

Finally, I am calm and can breathe deeper than I have in weeks. I have released the demons, the fear, the anger, the pain—all of it expelled into the universe and out of my mind, body, and soul. I am consoled. I am free.

HAVING THE ABILITY TO TAP INTO EMOTIONS in such an intense way is one of my many cherished gifts. Throughout each and every day, we take in so much that the range of events and emotions can sometimes overwhelm us. Some turn to drugs, alcohol, or sex to cope and to escape. These are the tools I used in the past to get through. Thank God I don't have to live like that anymore. I am free from that way of life. I can release back into the world all that I take in, the good and the bad. We are our experiences: They mold us, define us, and shape who we are. If we do not take care of ourselves and don't allow ourselves to grieve, laugh, and scream occasionally, we will crash and burn.

It is how we embrace our daily lives that determines what each day will bring. We hold such an immense power over our own destinies. That power scares people. It is so much easier to believe in luck or chance. The power for us is in how we react, how we interact, and how we embrace each moment. You cannot fully soak in the joy of today if your soul is full of yesterday's garbage. We need to expel all that we take in so we can face each new day cleansed.

PEOPLE OFTEN ASK HOW I CAN DO the work I do and how I have gotten through all that I have. How I have overcome sexual assault, rape, suicide attempts, deaths of loved ones, self-loathing, and the loss of my mother. How I can sit with families now as their loved ones die before them. How I can walk into strangers' homes and tell them their loved ones have just been murdered.

I believe that I am blessed beyond anything I could have imagined. I have seen so much death in my life, so much pain. It took me a long time to figure out how to deal with it all properly, productively. Now that I have, I believe I have been called upon by a Higher Power to walk others through their painful times.

I am no stranger to loss. I know what it feels like to have your heart burst out of your chest into tiny pieces, scattered and shattered. I know the strength it takes to muster a simple "Hello" and half-smile when you feel like you're dying inside. I also know how vital it is to take care of yourself and to allow yourself to grieve. I know how important it is to simply suit up and show up for life each day. In my past, I could not do that. I ran from everything; I never dealt with any of my feelings or emotions. I hid in dark barrooms and in smoke-filled places with other people just like me, all of us scared and running from life.

Today, I show up. I participate each and every day of my life. No matter how bad things get or how sad, mad, frustrated, scared, or angry I feel today, I have one certainty: Life will get better; I will not feel like this forever. Today the difference is that I acknowledge my feelings, I process them appropriately, and I deal with them.

Feelings are not facts, they are just that—feelings—and they won't kill you. Trust me! They come and go every second of our lives, and they can and will change at the drop of a hat. But you can face them if you show up for life, which means getting out of bed, getting dressed, going to work or school or wherever it is that you are expected to be that day. Get up and face life, because life is a gift and it is a short trip, my friend. We never know what day will be our last. It sounds like such a cliché, but it is one of the truest statements in life. We never know what is going to happen on any given day, and it is up to us to either face the day or run from it. You cannot let fear run the show. Walk through the fear and face the day, because you never know—today may be just like any other day or you may have the best day of your life. The difference will be that, no matter what, you will have fully experienced your day and not hidden from life.

There is an acronym called FEAR that I heard a while back, and it is one of my main mottos. You have two ways of looking at fear. You can either "Fuck Everything And Run" or "Face Everything And Recover." Today, I choose the latter.

Resources

I N THIS BOOK, I've dealt with many topics: alcoholism, drug abuse, sexual assault, and rape. My goal in sharing all this with you is to give you hope and show you that no matter where you have let life take you, no matter how dark it has become, there is light at the end of the tunnel. It's not always easy, because nothing worth fighting for ever is—and I am pretty sure that your life and your spirit are worth fighting for. Here are some good resources to help you on your road to recovery, whether you or a loved one needs the assistance.

Do you think you may have a drinking or drug problem?
This is a very common thought, and maybe you do and maybe you don't. It isn't my job, or anyone else's for that matter, to tell you whether you are an alcoholic or an addict. You must decide that on your own. If you are asking the question, then obviously some things have led you to this place, to this book, and to this very important question. This admission is a very personal one. On the road to recovery, which I hope follows, the admission is yours and yours alone. But here is the best part: You don't have to travel it alone. There are so many resources and

places to get help, and they are all at your fingertips. Here are but a few of them:

> Try **Alcoholics Anonymous** (hey, it won't kill ya): www.alcoholics-anonymous.org
>
> Check out the "Is AA for you?" section—it will answer every question you may have.

> Maybe **Narcotics Anonymous** is more your speed (pun intended): www.na.org

Also look in the Yellow Pages of your phone book for local phone numbers for AA and NA. People are there waiting to listen to you, help you, and even pick you up and take you to a meeting.

If you choose to go to a rehabilitation center, try Hazelden. Since 1949, the staff there has helped people reclaim their lives from the disease of addiction, using a variety of therapeutic approaches. It is a wonderful comprehensive center, and if it isn't right for you, the experts there can direct you to other resources or other centers.

www.hazelden.org

Do you think you may have an eating disorder?
Just like any other disease, an eating disorder is an addiction. Left untreated, it can lead to all kinds of problems, like liver damage, throat damage, and possibly death.

> The **National Eating Disorder Association** has great resources: www.edap.org/p.asp?WebPage_ID=337
>
> Or call its toll-free help-line to talk to someone in confidence: 1-800-931-2237.

Are you or a friend having suicidal thoughts?

This book dealt with not only my own battle with suicidal thoughts and attempts, but also my best friend taking her own life when I was only fifteen years old. I only wish there had been hotlines and resources back then like there are today. Maybe I would have picked up the phone and called someone. Suicide is no joke. If you are having these thoughts or you have a friend or loved one who has expressed these thoughts, call this number and talk to someone who is trained to help. Sometimes it is scary and hard to think about reaching out to someone who knows us or the people in our lives. That is why hotlines like these are available. They are free and confidential. You don't have to suffer in silence; there is help.

**Kristin Brooks Hope Center and its
National Hopeline Network**
1-800-SUICIDE (1-800-784-2433)
www.hopeline.com

National Suicide Prevention Lifeline
1–800–273–TALK (1–800–273–8255)
www.suicidepreventionlifeline.org

Are you a victim of a crime?

Do you know that as a crime victim you have many rights under the law? You have the right to be heard in the criminal justice process, to receive restitution, to be present at your trial or hearing, and to be treated with dignity, compassion, and respect. You also have rights to compensation, to protection, to a speedy trial, and to information about the status of your case. To learn more about your rights as a crime victim, check out these amazing resources:

The National Center for Victims of Crime
www.ncvc.org

Office for Victims of Crime
www.ovc.gov

Rape, Abuse & Incest National Network
www.rainn.org
   RAINN offers help that's free, confidential, and also available 24/7 through its National Sexual Assault Hotline: 1-800-656-HOPE (1-800-656-4673)

Are you wondering whether you are gay?
Whether you are just questioning your sexuality or you know for certain, it is helpful to reach out and find support. Things are so much better today for queer youth, but there are still many challenges, fears, acts of discrimination, and much hatred in this world. The goal is to keep you safe and to help you find an environment that will foster healthy questioning and development. Here are some wonderful places to look for help:

Gay, Lesbian and Straight Education Network
www.glsen.org

Human Rights Campaign
www.hrc.org

National Gay and Lesbian Task Force
www.thetaskforce.org

Blackout Girl

National Center for Transgender Equality
www.nctequality.org

Gender Public Advocacy Coalition
www.gpac.org

What can I do to help my adolescent child?
While all the above resources can help you as a parent, there is a great resource for parents by parents that can also offer a litany of resources:

By Parents for Parents
www.byparents-forparents.com

I hope you find these resources helpful, even if you aren't sure that you need help. There is no shame is seeking help. Life is hard and we go through so many ups and downs, especially as young people. Here is one certainty I can offer you as the best resource ever: *You never have to go through anything alone again.* Reach out, ask for help, and try something, anything *healthy*, that will help ease the pain or answer the questions.

With much love and respect,
Jennifer Storm

About the Author

Jennifer Storm is the Executive Director of the Victim/Witness Assistance Program in Harrisburg, Pennsylvania. In 2002, Governor Edward G. Rendell appointed Ms. Storm as a commissioner to the Pennsylvania Commission on Crime and Delinquency. Her media appearances include frequent live and taped appearances on all major networks as a spokesperson for victims' rights. She has been profiled and appeared in *We*, *Women*, *Central Penn Business Journal*, *Rolling Stone*, *TIME*, and many local and statewide newspapers. This is Ms. Storm's first book.

Other titles that may interest you:

A Place Called Self
Women, Sobriety, and Radical Transformation
Stephanie Brown, Ph.D.
With gentle guidance and personal stories, Brown helps
readers unravel painful truths and confusing feelings in
the process of weaving for themselves a true sense of self.
Softcover, 208 pp.
Order No. 2145

Get Me Out of Here
My Recovery from Borderline Personality Disorder
Rachel Reiland
This astonishingly honest memoir reveals what borderline
personality disorder feels like from the inside and how
recovery is possible. Softcover, 460 pp.
Order No. 2138

When Misery Is Company
End Self-Sabotage and Become Content
Anne Katherine
This fascinating and prescriptive book provides assistance
to clients who feel they might be making choices that keep
them miserable. Softcover, 304 pp.
Order No. 2158

Hazelden books are available at fine bookstores everywhere. To order directly from Hazelden, call 800-328-9000
or visit hazelden.org/bookstore.